INSEPARABLE

Five PERSPECTIVES
on SEX, LIFE, and LOVE
in DEFENSE of HUMANAE VITAE

*Edited by Todd Aglialoro
and Stephen Phelan*

INSEPARABLE

Five PERSPECTIVES
on SEX, LIFE, and LOVE
in DEFENSE of HUMANAE VITAE

Catholic
Answers
Press

Published by Catholic Answers, Inc.
2020 Gillespie Way
El Cajon, California 92020
1-888-291-8000 orders
619-387-0042 fax
catholic.com

Printed in the United States of America

Cover design by ebooklaunch.com
Interior design by Sherry Russell

978-1-68357-091-2
978-1-68357-092-9 Kindle
978-1-68357-093-6 ePub

In 1962, the Fathers of the Second Vatican Ecumenical Council were presented with drafts of the constitutions and decrees they were to discuss and vote upon. Most of these, with the exception of the document on the sacred liturgy, were famously eliminated from consideration during the first session of the council.

One of those eliminated from discussion was a dogmatic constitution entitled, "On Chastity, Matrimony, the Family, and Virginity." This document is barely mentioned in subsequent histories of the council, but today it bears close scrutiny. The hardy theologians of the Roman School, whom some of the prelates and *periti* from Northern Europe mocked and marginalized as out of touch with modern conditions, had produced a document that would have been of tremendous assistance to pastors of souls and Catholic thinkers, and one that in retrospect was prophetic and almost preternaturally precise about current challenges regarding human life and its cradle, the family. The discussion and approval of the document might have spared the Church so many trials!

Surely the memory of Bl. Pope Paul VI went back to those early days of the council with a certain regret as he was forced, in composing his great encyclical letter *Humanae Vitae*, to resolve a greater issue than that of "the pill." And, as his former admirers in various hierarchies of the Catholic world abandoned him, leaving him alone to fight for the truth, his old opponents of the Roman School, hitherto viewed as hidebound and outdated, were his clear supporters and friends. They prayed that he would maintain the clarity of the Ven. Pius XII, whose closest institutional associate he had been for over a decade. And he did.

What had they foreseen and addressed in the abandoned dogmatic constitution? Well, just about everything we take as normally controverted and discussed today. For example, already in 1962, they addressed sexual dysphoria and mutilation and the nature of sexual identity, sex education, same-sex attraction, the indissolubility of marriage, feminism, genetic manipulation, overpopulation and demographic shifts, and they dealt as well with contraception. Regarding which last, this would have been in the text of a proposed dogmatic constitution *Christifideles Universi*:

> This holy synod, while it most earnestly exhorts all that each and every one as far as possible effectively assist families who have a great number of children, at the same time severely reproves the recommending or the propagation of immoral means of contraceptives for limiting offspring, by which not only the good of the peoples is not defended, as is today sometimes falsely thought, but rather the whole social order is corrupted.[1]

Paul VI would have been mightily assisted had this or a similar text been promulgated by the council.

Had this fundamental declaration of the constant teaching of the Church in the matter of contraception been promulgated, then Paul VI's only task would have been to determine whether "the pill" actually constituted contraception or not. As it was, he had to defend the whole teaching of the Church, not just apply it in a particular matter of medical technology. There were at the time serious and respected theologians and philosophers, like the great Thomist Charles de Koninck, who erroneously did not see "the pill" as an unnatural means for the spacing of birth, but rather as acceptable in the context of marriage. But the genius of, or better, the onus on Papa Montini was his clear understanding that the whole issue had to be addressed explicitly and carefully. Thus, he gave to the Church the treasured and carefully crafted gift of *Humanae Vitae*, in which, in principle, the whole order of sexual morality is defended and explained.

Yes, he could have been spared the trouble by a preemptive decree of the council, but there is one sense in which the loving Providence of God may have permitted this politically or naïvely motivated omission. The original decree would have been in rather essentialist terms, minimally referring to the complexity and difficulty of human experience. What came to pass instead was the creation of a whole school of reflection, in large part lay, but significantly clerical too, that reflected more deeply on the concrete experience of human sexuality and married life.

Thus were born the reflections of Bishop Karol Wojtyla, and the personalist thought of Dietrich von Hildebrand and Josef Seifert and many others. Those who are more classically inclined Thomists might have done without the exhaustive analysis they offered, since they were already convinced, but it cannot be denied that an accidental but real benefit of the delay and of the ambiguities in *Gaudium et Spes* and in the work of the papal commission was to move serious Catholic thinkers outside the Roman School to expound and defend the traditional teaching in their own terms.

To no small extent, the diverse essays in this book demonstrate, and powerfully so, the good and meaning of this development.

Of course, the Church treasures and favors the classical teaching and approach of St. Thomas above all others, but her main concern is the salvation of souls. Any line of true reasoning and research that keeps souls from sin corresponds to her supreme law, which in the very last canon of the Code of Canon Law is defined as *salus animarum*: the salvation of souls. *Suprema lex salus animarum.*[2] But, in the case of contraception we are confronted with an especially deep application of this principle, for in order for there to be the salvation of souls, there have to be souls! Contraception, in the end, is a war against the glory of God shown forth in the procreation and education of human beings.

In this regard, it is important to make clear the relationship between a new evangelization regarding human life and the Church's teaching on contraception. Respect for human life is related essentially to respect for the integrity of marriage and the family. The attack on the innocent and defenseless life of the unborn has its origin in an erroneous view of human sexuality, which attempts to eliminate, by mechanical or chemical means, the essentially procreative nature of the conjugal act. This error maintains that the artificially altered act retains its integrity. The claim is that the act remains unitive or loving, even though the procreative nature of the act has been radically violated. In fact, it is not unitive, for one or both of the partners withholds an essential part of the gift of self, which is the essence of the conjugal union.

The manipulation of the conjugal act, as Paul VI courageously observed, has led to many forms of violence against marriage and family life.[3] Through the spread of the contraceptive mentality, especially among the young, human sexuality is no longer seen as the gift of God that draws a man and a woman together in a bond of lifelong and faithful love, crowned by the gift of new human life, but rather as a tool for personal gratification.[4] Once sexual union is no longer seen to be procreative by its very nature, human sexuality is abused in ways that are profoundly harmful and indeed destructive of individuals and of society. One has only to think of the devastation daily wrought in our world by the multi-billion-dollar industry of pornography, or of the aggressive homosexual agenda that can only result in the profound unhappiness and even despair of those affected by it and in the destruction of society. Fundamental to the transformation of culture is the proclamation of the truth about the conjugal union in its fullness and the correction of the contraceptive thinking that fears procreation; that fears life.

In today's secular culture, there is a confusion about the meaning of human sexuality that is reaping a harvest of profound personal unhappiness often to the point of the breakdown of the family, of the corruption of children and young people, and, ultimately, of self-destruction. Disordered sexual activity, sexual activity outside of marriage, and the constant and potent false messages, served up by the communications media, about who we are as man and woman, are the signs of a desperate need of a new evangelization. Christians are called to witness to the distinct gifts of man and woman to be placed at the service of God and his holy people through a chaste life. Christian marriage is the primary locus of that critical witness. Through sound marital and family life our culture will be transformed. Without sound marital and family life, it will never be transformed.

It is instructive to note that Pope Benedict XVI, in his

encyclical letter *Caritas in Veritate*, made special reference to *Humanae Vitae*, underscoring its importance "for delineating the *fully human meaning of the development that the Church proposes*" (15)[5] Benedict went on to make clear that the teaching in *Humanae Vitae* is not simply a matter of "individual morality," declaring:

> *Humanae Vitae* indicates the *strong links between life ethics and social ethics*, ushering in a new area of magisterial teaching that has gradually been articulated in a series of documents, most recently John Paul II's encyclical letter *Evangelium Vitae*.[6]

In treating the question of procreation, Benedict underscored the critical importance of the right understanding of human sexuality, marriage and the family. He wrote:

> The Church, in her concern for man's authentic development, urges him to have full respect for human values in the exercise of his sexuality. It cannot be reduced merely to pleasure or entertainment, nor can sex education be reduced to technical instruction aimed solely at protecting the interested parties from possible disease or the "risk" of procreation. This would be to impoverish and disregard the deeper meaning of sexuality, a meaning which needs to be acknowledged and responsibly appropriated not only by individuals but also by the community (44).[7]

The restoration of respect for the integrity of the conjugal act is essential to the future of any culture, to the advancement of a culture of life. In the words of Benedict XVI, it is necessary "once more to hold up to future generations the beauty of marriage and the family, and the fact that these institutions correspond to the deepest needs and dignity of the person"[8]

Correspondingly, Benedict noted, "States are called to *enact policies promoting the centrality and integrity of the family* founded on marriage between a man and a woman, the primary vital cell of society, and to assume responsibility for its economic and fiscal needs, while respecting its essentially relational character" (44).[9]

The *Catechism of the Catholic Church* reminds us that "[s]o-called *moral permissiveness* rests on an erroneous conception of human freedom" and that "the necessary precondition for the development of true freedom is to let oneself be educated in the moral law" (2526). As is clear from the above considerations, individual freedom and the freedom of society in general depend upon a fundamental education in the truth about human sexuality and the exercise of that truth in a pure and chaste life. The *Catechism* goes on to observe: "Those in charge of education can reasonably be expected to give young people instruction respectful of the truth, the qualities of the heart, and the moral and spiritual dignity of man." For the Christian, this entails education in holiness of life and in the respect owed to the inviolable dignity of self, body and soul, and of others as one's self. The teaching in the matter of contraception that Paul VI set forth in *Humanae Vitae,* which Benedict XVI strongly confirms, is in fact the perennial teaching of the Church.

Yes, the vicissitudes of the council and its undoubted historical limitations still lead a number of "progressives" to imagine that the Church's perennial teaching on chastity, matrimony, the family, and virginity can be changed. Fifty

years of the pontifical magisterium after the council have
made it abundantly clear, however, that even though the
would-be dogmatic constitution dealing these matters never
appeared, the teaching Church has nonetheless held firm on
every point. May God grant that our present Holy Father,
who, on the occasion of the beatification of Pope Paul VI,
thanked him for his "for humble and prophetic witness of
love for Christ and his Church,[10] may in the end disappoint
the partisans of innovation and of submission to the spirit of
the world as deeply as he did.

† *Raymond Leo Cardinal Burke*

~

Contents

The Truth Is One

Stephen Phelan

It was a brutal road. Father Jonathan did what he could to navigate the groaning Land Cruiser between the trenches and holes in the red dirt, but the pounding took a physical toll on all of us. Our small crew was on a ten-day swing through Tanzania and Uganda, seeking to confirm reports of women suffering crippling side effects from long-acting reversible contraceptives (LARCs), and the trip had laid bare the hopelessness of some of the women harmed by the West's technological "solution" to "overpopulation." (Some people think that population control in the developing world is a thing of the past. It's not: it has simply been rebranded as "reproductive health" and integrated into legitimate development and aid work.)

For whatever reason, our last stop in a tiny village southwest of Mbale, Uganda was the hardest. The stories were the same as those we'd heard in more than a dozen other cities and villages: a mother of two is told that in order to get out of poverty, she needs to "space pregnancies," which requires a shot, or an implant in her upper arm, or a strange device inserted in her uterus. When weeks, months, or years later she becomes anemic and can't work, loses her libido, bleeds profusely, suffers debilitating headaches and any number of other ill effects, it is a mystery. Maybe she is cursed—as such maladies are traditionally explained. Her husband beats her, throws her out of her home, and takes up with another woman who wants sex and who can work. She has no legal recourse, no doctor down the street to whom she can speak about her symptoms, no Walgreens at the corner where she can at least get something for the pain. The local clinic, which sterilized her for free, now wants several months' salary to reverse the procedure.

There were less dramatic stories as well, of course, but what emerged over those ten days was a particular theme: almost none of the hundreds of women we met were warned of the consequences of the method they "chose." We interviewed an obstetrician who had been brought to a small hospital near Tororo by Human Life International, with whom I was working. He told us of how many women he has treated who were given Depo-Provera shots *while pregnant*, since those giving these treatments had very little training. The quota-driven "RH (reproductive health) teams" conducted no examinations or interviews, and were incentivized to give out as many "units" as possible of whatever contraceptive technology they happened to have on hand.

This is what "reproductive health" looks like far from the skyscraping offices of American non-governmental organizations and the United Nations. The Church's teaching on contraception isn't exactly popular in such lofty quarters, from which billions are invested to make contraception the *sine qua non* of "development."

Closer to home, hosting marriage enrichment conferences around the country as my colleagues and I do with the St. John Paul II Foundation, we hear different stories: not about coerced sterilization, but about family breakdown; not about women left sick and abandoned, but about spouses who, despite being faithful and wanting a happy, healthy marriage, have for lack of formation been left on their own to negotiate the potholed and dangerous roads of our contraceptive society. Despite our comfort and security, our sense of freedom in the West has become so misshapen that we have unlearned many basic human truths, and so are mystified to find ourselves more and more isolated, choosing counterfeit goods while leaving the greatest goods unapproached.

When we see a family that radiates joy and simplicity, we wonder how we can get "that." Or how we can get that *back*.

Humanae Vitae (HV) is just one document from the Catholic Church's body of social and moral doctrine, which together presents a unified series of claims and arguments about the true flourishing of every human person and every society. To many Catholics today, parts of that doctrine—especially those dealing with sex and marriage—are an inconvenience or an embarrassment. But when I hear complaints in Scottsdale or Tampa about how the Church's teaching on life, family, and sexuality is "out of touch" with the world today I think of the women we met in Uganda and Tanzania. I realize that even in the cities and suburbs of the wealthiest nation in history, *we still get basic things very wrong.*

In this book's essay from Shaun and Jessica McAfee, we find a common story of how moral incoherence around fertility can infect even the intentions of faithful Christians. That young women have for decades been put on "the pill" for a bizarrely wide range of reasons doesn't seem to strike anyone as strange. Even well-intentioned parents and chaste daughters push through the awkward conversations and trips to the pharmacy, as underlying health problems are pharma-cologically hidden and everyone ritually repeats, without be-lieving, that being on the pill doesn't really change anything.

Yet it is also not an uncommon story to see the Church's "strange" teaching on marriage and sexuality end up being, as it was for Jessica and Shaun, a reason to become Catholic. And as is often the case with such converts, they came in swinging: on fire for the truth of Catholicism and its wit-ness to life.

Pope Benedict made the point memorably in his encycli-cal *Caritas in Veritate*:

> *Only in truth does charity shine forth*, only in truth can charity be authentically lived. Truth is the light that gives meaning and value to charity. That light is both the light of reason and the light of faith, through which the intellect attains to the natural and supernatural truth of charity: it grasps its meaning as gift, acceptance, and communion. Without truth, charity degenerates into sentimentality. Love be-comes an empty shell, to be filled in an arbitrary way (3).

Standing in truth when the world goes crazy is both a powerful witness and an occasion for serious people of good faith to come together in understanding. In Allan C. Carl-son's essay we hear a voice from outside the Catholic Church expressing profound gratitude for the stand that Pope Paul VI took with HV, a stand that the Church continues to hold even as most of the world descends once again into pagan-ism. Few are as qualified as Carlson to connect the histories of the Roman Empire into which Christianity was born with the histories of Catholic Christianity and various col-lapses of Protestantism on contraception, and both of these with the reams of social-science data showing what happens when the idea becomes widely accepted that sex and procreation can be separated:

> In 2018 the once-Christian "Western nations" have sped well beyond what even the most sex-obsessed Roman pagan could have imagined. To see a world in near-absolute moral and sexual darkness, a contemporary Western witness need merely open his eyes and look around.

Carlson also thoroughly debunks the lingering argument from John T. Noonan's 1965 book *Contraception* that the Church's historical condemnation was based on a reaction to various threats inside and outside the early Church rather than a clear understanding of human sexuality. No, Carlson insists: the Church was right then, as it is now. Human nature and the law written on every human heart have not changed, because they cannot change.

Explaining in philosophical terms why this stubbornly remains true, Paul Gondreau of Providence College presents a fresh and challenging natural-law defense of HV. As the cultural wreckage recounted by Carlson attests, the fundamental error is separating moral and ethical truths from the physical world and its natural reality:

> As man "is" a body-soul composite unity, so his actions "ought" to respect his fundamental structure, at least if he wishes to attain his proper flourishing and happiness. He does this in the sexual arena by honoring the procreative-unitive nature of sex. Further, while we can, and must, distinguish the procreative (as expressive of the body) from the unitive or personalist (as expressive of the intellectual soul), we can no more separate these two than separate body from soul.

Truth is one. The view of the human person presented throughout this book, and highlighted in Gondreau's chapter, is the Church's long-held position that man is both body and soul—not merely a mind that controls a body. The latter "Cartesianist" anthropology divorces man in his nature in an act of pure will that, over time, turns man against himself and others. We cannot build anything good or sustainable on a bad metaphysics or a bad anthropology any more than we can build a house on sand.

The divorce between mind and body in the view of human nature is no secondary concern. Descartes's attractive but catastrophic error came at a time when fracturing was all the rage: more than a century after Luther's rebellion and just over a century after St. Thomas More was executed for refusing to sanction King Henry VIII's divorce. Wars between Christians raged throughout Europe, and the Church's bungled (but grossly misunderstood) response to Galileo's intransigence led Descartes to seek a new basis for knowledge where Church authority could not intrude. The result cleaved scientific knowledge from theological knowledge, injecting subjectivity into truth claims that had traditionally been understood as objective and real.

One need not be a professor of philosophy to see how this follows from the divorce between body and mind, any more than one need be a sociologist to see the harm this error continues to inflict on us today. It's telling that people on all sides of this debate recognize that the advent of the Enlightenment and its new basis for scientific knowledge and for technology was a crucial turning point for Western society. Depending on your perspective, it was the beginning of progress, or the beginning of the end.

Like Gondreau, moral theologian Mark Latkovic of Sacred Heart Major Seminary pinpoints the idolatry of technology as an effect of confusion over the nature of the human person, showing how the Church in and after HV responded, with a new and robust personalism, to critics who thought that advances in science somehow presented a new understanding of the human person that demanded a change in doctrine on contraception.

To discuss personalism in the context of Catholic doctrine is obviously to turn the spotlight to Pope St. John Paul II, who not only consulted with Paul VI in the creation of HV but, as Paul's successor, became its most powerful and most authoritative defender. Pope Paul's strong defense of the Church's traditional understanding of marriage and sexuality is all the more remarkable when one considers, as Latkovic does, the storms buffeting the Church in that era: everything from nihilistic pop culture to the emergence of an intensely skeptical academe. He draws a fascinating parallel between the competing and contemporaneous revolutions in science and sexuality that defined the era, from the moon landing to the Pill, leading to the popular but irrational belief that because of such remarkable scientific advancements, social advancements via science were also, necessarily, right around the corner. The fruits of this belief were painfully evident to us years later in the villages of Uganda and Tanzania.

Latkovic reminds us that our best response is not a theory or an insight, but a Person:

[Jesus] provides the ultimate standard of the perfect man and morally upright action. This is why John Paul was so fond of a particular passage from the Vatican II document, *Gaudium et Spes*: "The truth is that only in the mystery of the incarnate Word does the mystery of man take on light. For Adam, the first man, was a figure of him who was to come [cf. Rom. 5:14], namely, Christ the Lord. Christ, the final Adam, by the revelation of the mystery of the Father and his love, fully reveals man to man himself and makes his supreme calling clear." Even an issue such as contraception can only be given a satisfactory answer in light of Christ's redemption of the body.

In Jesus Christ, the Logos, through whom all things were created, we find our origin and destiny. We also find, unsurprisingly, an inner unity to creation in both its being and its behavior, in both its *is* and its *ought*. Such natural realities track perfectly with a Creator who is himself a communion of love, a perpetual and perfect being and act of pure gift, three persons in one God.

It is a strength of this work that each author turns to the Bible at crucial points in his arguments. As biblical scholar Joseph Atkinson shows, the biblical support for HV is indeed strong. In his Theology of the Body, St. John Paul II relied heavily on key scriptural passages to build an anthropological basis for his teaching on sexual morality. Such crucial passages include the first two chapters of Genesis, Matthew 19, and the letters of St. Paul, but Atkinson also develops a parallel case based on rabbinic texts that enlighten the traditional understanding of the Bible on these questions as well as lesser-known Bible passages that reveal God's intent with regard to grace, agency, and salvation on these questions.

Atkinson makes a powerful case for returning to Sacred Scripture as a necessary complement to natural law, the magisterium, and others sources for understanding the purpose and meaning of human sexuality:

We have entertained a long theological amnesia about the pedagogical value of a divinely willed creation. Our emphasis on the human subjective experience, coupled with the value of human freedom, has sometimes caused us to mute the voice of creation. . . . [T]here is an integrity to the act of sexual communion that begins a process, the structure of which man has no authority to pervert, and that must always be respected and must be allowed its full development once begun. *Humanae Vitae* takes this into full account when it condemns "every action which, either in anticipation of the conjugal act, or in its accomplishment, or in the development of its natural consequences, proposes, whether as an end or as a means, to render procreation impossible" (14).

This point is very important: The Church does not condemn a pill, a chemical, or a piece of latex. What is condemned is the *contraceptive act*—the choice of a person to deliberately thwart the procreative end of the sexual act. A pill that has a contraceptive effect may have another effect that makes it useful in healing; an object that can be used to prevent pregnancy may have another, morally good use. A person who commits what the Church calls the "grave sin" of contraception can seek forgiveness in the sacrament of reconciliation and resolve to amend his life accordingly. But the act is, as the Church has said many times at multiple levels of authority, "intrinsically evil."

Many find this teaching difficult to bear. Couples can find natural fertility awareness methods, based on periodic abstinence, challenging to practice. Some Catholics long to be faithful to the teaching, but live with a spouse who is unsupportive. Women with reproductive or other health problems may find themselves steered by doctors toward easy contraceptive solutions. Such situations are as varied and numerous as there are marriages, and people in them need help.

Faithful Christians in medicine must continue to look for innovative means to improve genuine healing in reproductive health, and the Church must support those who feel left out of the public debate. Couples who find the teaching true and have integrated prayer into marital life should remember and pray for other couples, especially those who feel trapped by circumstances beyond their control. Although they can make no claim to change the Church's teaching, which is based on unchangeable truths of the human person, such difficulties demand continuous pastoral attention.

I have been asked if the Church's teaching on sexuality is based on natural law, on biblical grounds, on personal narratives, or on social science. I always have the same answer: *yes*. Or, to be more precise, it is based on truth itself, which of course is revealed from many sources and in many disciplines. Those who accuse the Church of "physicalism," of resting the entire case on human biology, miss or ignore the Church's theological, scriptural, and historical case. Those who demand one and only one line of evidence—the airtight prooftext or syllogism—as a condition for assent will be edified to see the teaching presented instead as a rich mosaic of truth.

So is the Church's teaching in HV doctrinal, historical, or theological? Is it based on natural law, the Church's own authority, or on factors outside its authority, such as medical and social science? Should it be considered social doctrine or moral doctrine? Is it about personal responsibility or about social responsibility?

The answer to all these questions is the same: *yes*. The truth of the teaching is what matters, and its components are inseparable. Though we may arrive at this truth from a diversity of roads, some of them as jarring as the one we traversed in Uganda, they lead to the same destination. The roads leading away from the truth may seem new and smooth underfoot; yet their destination is desolation.

Love and Truth are united at their Source. Man and woman joined in sacramental marriage cannot be separated until death. One cannot divorce the procreative from the unitive end of the marital act without rejecting God's design for the person and the family. This is true for women and men in Dar es Salaam and Kampala, in Los Angeles and Toronto, in Oslo, Madrid, Moscow, and São Paolo.

That such truths are undeniable does not stop many from denying them, but even the most powerful of these cannot forestall forever the consequences of such denial, and the bill is coming due today. It is an act of love to tell this truth, as the Church has not only these fifty tumultuous years since *Humanae Vitae,* but since its own conception two millennia ago. Staying true to this teaching, and finding new ways to reach those who find it difficult or impossible to believe, is the task before us.

~

1

"Let Man Not Separate"

Joseph C. Atkinson

The Church must get a clearer idea of what it really is in the mind of Jesus Christ as recorded and preserved in Sacred Scripture and in Apostolic Tradition, and interpreted and explained by the tradition of the Church under the inspiration and guidance of the Holy Spirit. Provided we implore the aid of the Spirit and show Him a ready obedience, He will certainly never fail to redeem Christ's promise: "But the Paraclete, the Holy Ghost, whom the Father will send in my name, he will teach you all things and bring all things to your mind, whatsoever I shall have said to you."
　　—Bl. Paul VI, *Ecclesiam Suam*, 1964

In his first encyclical, Pope Paul VI called on his brother bishops to do their best in serving the Church during a time of great tumult and great moment. After he inherited the Second Vatican Council from his predecessor, that meeting of the world's bishops had taken on a life of its own, and the new pontiff wanted to set a course in line with John XXIII's intentions and the entire history of great councils in the two millennia of the Church he now led.

Over the next four years, Paul would propagate six more encyclicals, the most consequential of which would be his last, *Humanae Vitae* (HV), released in July 1968. It has been reported widely that the rebellion that followed its release so dismayed the Holy Father that he did not again attempt to release an encyclical for the remaining years of his pontificate. It would be left to his successor, John Paul II, to reinforce the teaching of HV, both with the full magisterial weight of his office and with a remarkable series of papal audiences which later became known as the Theology of the Body.

In his great, broad, and innovative theological opus, John Paul deepened the theological vocabulary of the Church in considering the lived perspective of the human person in all its wonder and portent. Key to these meditations were certain scriptural passages that, in John Paul's analyses, brought to light the truth of the human person made in the image of the Triune God who made him. Focusing on the nature of creation and on an anthropology ordered to and participating in God's own holiness reveals a strong scriptural foundation for the truth of HV.

Although my approach is different from that taken by John Paul II, I hope this analysis will complement his profound work that we have only begun to unpack and will inform those who recognize, as did St. Jerome, that the Word of God is the "soul of theology (*Dei Verbum* 24) and the foundation for all that the Church believes and teaches.

I. How Does Revelation Work?

In asking the question, "What does the Bible say about *x*?" Christians appeal to Scripture as an authority that they believe reveals God's will. The resulting problem is not about authority, as most Christians assume that the Bible is authoritative, but about interpretation. How does the biblical text make its teaching known? Or, to be more precise: *how does God authoritatively reveal his binding truth in and through his written word?*

People tend to think of the Bible as a book containing propositions that can be easily isolated and consulted for clear, binding answers. To some degree, this approach grew out of the Protestant Reformers' doctrine on the perspicacity of Scripture—the idea that all things necessary to salvation are "clearly propounded and opened in some place of Scripture . . . that not only the learned, but the unlearned . . . may attain unto a sufficient understanding of them."[11]

The strength of this position is that it allows for divine truth (a transcendent reality) to exist within the created order and proposes an authoritative guide for human actions. That is, it takes serious the fact that the God of the Judeo-Christian heritage is a God who communicates and reveals himself. The weakness of this approach is that it *tends* toward a univocity regarding what can be considered as binding truth. Only teaching that is clear, direct, and unambiguously comprehended (by the learned or unlearned) has binding authority. If any issue is not directly discerned, then there is no authoritative guidance and believers are free to do as they wish.

But is this the way revelation actually works? Clearly, Scripture contains prescriptive formulae that appear to fit the clear-and-direct description. The Ten Commandments are the preeminent example of this unambiguous form of teaching. But even here we find a problem. For example, the third commandment (Exod. 20:8–11) teaches that the Sabbath must be kept holy and that no work be done on it. Yet within Judaism there is a long tradition over the generations of discussing which human activities constitute *work*.

One rabbinical discussion discusses the question of wicking. If a person tanned leather or dyed wool for a living, would he be allowed to begin the process just before Friday sunset? The rabbinical house of Hillel ruled that as long as the man's own actions in this regard were finished by sundown, he was not breaking the Sabbath. The rabbinical house of Shammai ruled contrariwise, implying that by putting the leather in the dye vat directly before the Sabbath, the man had *started a process of absorption* that continued over into the Sabbath and thus violated the Sabbath law.[12]

Similarly, the early Church was split over the question of the Mosaic requirements in relationship to salvation in Christ. Their struggle was over rightly interpreting the action of God and the sacred texts. The "party of circumcision" took the position that to be saved in Christ, one had to become a Jew, keep the law (symbolized by the act of circumcision), and then follow Jesus' salvific way (Acts 15:5). They had strong scriptural support in Genesis 17, which spoke of the perduring covenant of circumcision. The second group, saying one only needed to trust the work of Jesus, could also appeal to Scripture (e.g., the new covenant in Jeremiah 31:31; the new Mosaic covenant in Deuteronomy 18:5; and the Suffering Servant of Isaiah 53). This group, which included St. Paul, maintained that salvation was predicated not on any work of the law but only on the work of Christ.

Here we find two contradictory interpretations of God's work and word. Clearly, appealing to scriptural texts or experience alone did not resolve the matter. Instead, the New Testament records, "the apostles and the elders were gathered together to consider this matter" and there was "much debate" (Acts 15:6–7).

The astonishing claim of the Church, even in its nascent form, was that it could come to know the mind of God and to declare to the whole Church definitive and binding decisions. This first conciliar meeting of the Church delivered its conclusions to fellow Christians by saying: "it has seemed good to the Holy Spirit and to us" (Acts 15:28). In this way, salvation could be known securely by all.

From this we see that the Scripture witnesses to the need for both the sacred texts *and* their divinely willed *interpretative matrix* (the authoritative teaching charism of the Church) to be able to apprehend the truth contained in them.

A Biological Lesson for Exegesis

This intrinsic and organic unity between Word Inscribed, Word Incarnated, and Word as Interpreter can be seen through an analogy taken from the world of embryology. When human sperm and egg unite, there is present in the zygote *all* the DNA constitutive of the human person, which amounts to around *ten to the power of eleven* (10^{11}) bits of information.[13] That's a lot of information! As Jerome Lejeune put it, to write out all the DNA information in the zygote letter by letter would require all the letters contained in five *Encyclopedia Britannicas* to be set side by side.

But all this information would remain isolated and unusable without a reader and interpreter. To carry out this interpretive task would require an interpretive mechanism with perhaps a thousand to a million times *more* bits of information.[14] Although in genetic science the human genome has to a great degree been "decoded" and is being interpreted and even manipulated, all this complexity is present in a basic work of God's design, evidenced in the development of every human person from conception to adulthood.

Microscopically, the DNA information is intrinsically bound to its own organic interpretive matrix so that it can literally become "incarnate" in the person. Without this information *and* the biological instrument of interpretation, there is no human person. Macroscopically, divine truth, which is given in God's written word, is intrinsically bound to its own organic interpretative matrix: the Body of Christ, the Church that alone allows for the word's full "decoding." Without this information *and* the ecclesial interpretative matrix, there is no salvific teaching for the people of God.

The lack of such an authority in Protestantism can be seen in its approach to contraception. A large number of Protestants assume that the morality of contraception has always been just a "Catholic issue," but this is simply false. Prior to the Anglican Communion's Lambeth Conference of 1930, the *unanimous* and *unbroken* Protestant teaching, drawn from Scripture, was that contraception use is gravely immoral. Since then, in the absence of an ecclesial interpretive voice to function as a reminder, there has been a worsening magisterial amnesia within the Protestant world regarding its historic scriptural teaching.[15]

There is also an underlying judgment often made by modern Christian ethicists that previous understandings of human sexuality and morality are basically physicalistic, with little or no appreciation for human subjectivity or freedom. To return for a moment to our embryological metaphor, they want to denucleate the *revelational zygote* of all its information and replace it with modernity's own developed information package, governed by the priority for human subjectivity. Or, to use a computer analogy, these ethicists would change the operating system of the computer from one based on biblical and traditional principles to one that prioritizes human perspective and experience. It's a radically different way of proceeding, an epistemological break with the past that conceives of the human person in a radically different way from that presented by Scripture.

II. The Evidence of Ancient Israel

The first three chapters of Genesis provide the *principles* for a biblical anthropology. These principles enable Christians to make a comprehensive moral determination about contraceptive behavior within the sexual act.

The Idea of History

The first words of God's revelation to Israel undid the foundations of the pagan conception of the world and its understanding of man. "In the beginning, God created" implies there is also a purpose or *telos* for this creation.[16] Previously, pagan religions had been tied to the recurring agricultural cycles of nature. There were multiple gods, plus impersonal fates with even greater power than the gods. Man was a helpless creature, at the mercy of all these competitive forces. With the Hebrew revelation, the linear nature of time became fundamental to the biblical narrative—life now had a beginning that moved toward a conclusion. Events in time had meaning because they could be evaluated in terms of their relationship to the *telos*, the end purpose. Thus, *personal human acts* took on a profound meaning and became part of the salvific process.[17] What the individual human person does, mattered.

God the Creator

Genesis creates an *absolute* division between that which is created and that which creates. In Hebrew, only God can be the subject of the verb "to create" (*barah*). Hence, all created reality is contingent upon God for its being. This differs radically from pagan myths in which the gods themselves are created.[18]

It is important to note that God first creates an inchoate, formless mass (*tohu vevohu*—Gen. 1:2). This is an original *unity,* into which God successively speaks. With each divine word, each earthly creation emerges from it. God's word provides the structure and purpose of each thing within the complex of creation. *Thus, the intelligibility of creation can only be found in God and not in the creature.* Once again, any moral evaluation has to take this into account.

The Nature of Man

The first three chapters of Genesis lay out the foundational anthropology that informs Judeo-Christian culture. Man's uniqueness is signaled by the fact that God stops the process of creation, and we are presented with the Creator's inner dialogue. He desires to create a being who carries a form of transcendence within his nature, and so he makes man in his own image. The magnitude of this is hardly conceivable.

To know the nature of the human person, we must refer back to the nature of God. His inner dialogue as presented ("let *us* make man in *our* image") bears witness to some form of inner communion within God. The name used for God (*'elohim*) is a *plural* form, but is only used with the *singular* verb. This double sense clearly produces a tension, particularly as the heart of Jewish revelation centers on the concept of God being one (*'echad*—Deut. 6:4). In fact, the word *'echad* can help us to resolve this tension, as it has the sense of diversity in unity.

For example, in Genesis 1:5 we read: "There was evening and there was morning, one day (*'echad*)." Clearly, the *one* day was made up of both the evening and the morning. In Genesis 2:24, man *and* woman become one (*'echad*) flesh.

So, the oneness of God does allow for some sense of otherness, of some form of communion to exist within him. This becomes the key for unpacking the image-bearing nature of man. Like God, in his essence man is a being of *communion*.

This idea of communion is reinforced in Genesis 1:27: "God created man in his own image, in the image of God he created him; male and female he created them." There are several peculiarities about this short verse. First, the verb *barah* ("create") is used three times, indicating man's unique creation. Bearing the divine image, man becomes the iconic representative of God in creation. Importantly, this is the first mention of gender: "Male and female he created them." Earlier, when God commands the animals to be fruitful and multiply (Gen. 1:22), there is no mention of gender, yet clearly it is required. In this text, gender therefore functions at a higher level in the human person and is linked with man's being in the divine image.

"Be Fruitful and Multiply"

After the creation of the man and woman, the first commandment is given: "And God blessed them, and God said to them, 'Be fruitful and multiply'" (Gen. 1:28). The Hebraic word for *blessing* signifies "abundance." Hence to be blessed is to have much land, many cattle, many children, etc. Thus there is a connection between God's love—his blessing—and procreation: "He will love you, bless you, and multiply you; he will also bless the fruit of your body" (Deut. 7:13). Accordingly, "there shall not be male or female barren among you" (v.14).

As Michael Kaufman notes: "In Judaism procreation is a major—if not *the* major—purpose of the sexual act; the reproductive organs were created for generation."[19] This becomes one of the two major principles in Judaism that determine the morality of a sexual act. Our physical body is ordered to a *telos*.

Rabbinical texts over the centuries have attested to this. The *Shulchan Aruch* (1563), probably the most foundational of all Jewish code books, states: "Every man is obliged to marry in order to fulfill the duty of procreation, and whoever does not is as if he had shed blood, diminished the image of God, and caused the holy presence to depart from Israel."[20]

One-Fleshness

Genesis 1:27 states that "in the image of God he created *him,* male and female he created *them*" (emphasis added). This tension between the singular and plural is only resolved in the next chapter, which details the process of man's creation. Even though man had a perfect relationship with God in Eden, there is still something missing; he is alone. Being in the image of *God-who-is-communion*, the male needs the female for fulfillment. It is critical to biblical anthropology that instead of creating the female as a separate and autonomous person, God uses the substance (the rib) of the first man (2:21–22) to build the woman. When God presents the woman, the man exclaims this is "bone of my bones and flesh of my flesh" (2:23).

This way of bringing forth the human creation is the foundation of anthropology, and this vitally informs human sexuality. The key is the one-flesh union that is predicated on an original primordial unity that *existed in the one before the two were created*. It is not the union of two autonomous and indifferent persons. The two already possess an indissoluble relationship because she is bone of his bones and flesh of his flesh. In becoming one flesh, they experience the original primal unity of man. The original man receives the other who is from him and becomes whole. The woman comes from man and goes back to him. In marriage their oneness in flesh becomes an ever-giving and -receiving of each other in one organic unity.

As we shall see, the theological purpose of this one-flesh communion in the order of creation is to be reflective of the inner communion (i.e., the oneness) of God in the divine order. In the divine economy, communion in God takes the form of the indissoluble and infinite relationship of love between the Father, Son, and Holy Spirit. In the created order, this communion takes the form of the one-flesh union of man and woman, which is meant to be iconic of the tri-person unity in God.[21] *In this way, the one-flesh union (symbolized in the sexual embrace) takes its structure and meaning from the oneness of God.*

Only within this framework can an adequate moral evaluation of any sexual act be made.[22] If an intentional act prevents or perverts the unitive meaning of the sexual act, then the transcendent capacity of the human sexual act and its ability to image forth and participate in the unitive nature of God is attacked and damaged.

Holiness

The second chapter of Genesis operates on two levels simultaneously. First, it understands the gift of sexuality as an overcoming of loneliness through the one-flesh union (v.18). The second level more subtly reveals the theological structure of human sexuality: sexual union is a reflection of, and participation in, the communion within God. This chapter is filled with terms and symbols that are evocative of the temple, the cult, and the covenant:[23] the use of the covenantal name for God (Yahweh); the eastward position of Eden (like the Jerusalem temple); and the mention of gold (which covered the *sancta* of the temple), bdellium (used to describe manna in the ark), and onyx stone (used in the breastplate of the high priest). Eden had the Tree of Life and the temple had a stylized menorah that was shaped like a tree. Several words are clearly cultic: the command to work (*avodah*) and to keep (*shamrah*) in 2:15 are technical terms used in reference to the Torah and covenant; the word *tardemah* (deep sleep) which the man enters when the rib to be removed (2:21) is also used for the covenantal sleep Abraham enters when he receives the covenant from God (Gen. 15:12).

We can summarize our findings so far:

1) Man is made in the image of God;
2) this image means he is made for communion;
3) this communion is given a concrete form in the male-female relationship;
4) communion is given a privileged expression in the one-flesh union;
5) therefore, man's one-flesh union is both this-worldly and intrinsically linked to God in his inner unity (communion) and life (fecundity).

Conception and the Child

Scripture bears uniform witness that the gift of conception and a child within a marital union are always seen as a gift of which the Lord, himself, is the agent and initiator. Conception was determined by the Lord and is a reproduction of the image of God. Eve, at the birth of Cain, says, "I have gotten a man with the help of the LORD" (Gen. 4:1). Jacob makes the point to Rachel: "Am I in the place of God, who has withheld from you the fruit of the womb?" (Gen. 30:2). The Lord himself says, "*Shall I who allow her to conceive*, yet close her womb?" (Isa. 66:9, emphasis added).

Scripture also understands that the Lord is active *before* and *after* conception. The Lord says, "Before I formed you in the womb I knew you" (Jer. 1:5). At the same time, God knows the future vocation of each person: "In thy book were written . . . the days that were formed for me, when as yet there was none of them" (Ps. 139:16).

In Scripture, God determines a man's life and its purpose *before*, *during*, and *after* conception. Positively willing to remove the possibility of procreation in the sexual act, then, not only contradicts God's design for our bodily union—it removes the agency of God from the marital embrace. As with the rest of creation, we are stewards of the transmission of human life, not its arbiter.

Holiness as Absolute

Now we come to the key criterion for the evaluation of *any* behavior within the people of God. When God established the Mosaic covenant, he declared that the existence of his chosen people was predicated on holiness. "You shall be to me a kingdom of priests and a holy nation" (Exod. 19:6). In Semitic thought, *only God is holy*. People and things can only have a derivative holiness by cohering to and participating in God's own absolute holiness.[24] Without this holiness, covenantal Israel would cease to exist.

Many of the laws of the Torah that determine which behaviors are connatural with or are hostile to God's holiness deal with human sexuality. The ancient rabbinical texts *Berachot* and *Levitcus Rabbah* show how the Jewish communities over the centuries understood that sexual activity and holiness were interrelated:

Why is the section in the Torah on forbidden sexual relations juxtaposed to the scripture readings of *K'doshim*,

Holy Ones? To teach you that everywhere you find a fence preventing transgression of the sexual laws, you find holiness . . . Whoever distances himself from violating the sexual laws is called holy.[25]

These ancient texts (fourth to sixth centuries A.D.) are referring to the Holiness Code in Leviticus 17–26. This section is structured around one phrase: "You shall be holy to me; for I the LORD am holy, and have separated you from the peoples" (Lev. 20:26). This appears several times and, what is unusual for the Torah, gives the reason for these laws. The individual actions of the Israelites, particularly sexual actions, must be holy or Israel will be in an immoral state that contradicts God's holiness. To be God's people our willful acts must cohere with the holiness of God.

Anthropologist Mary Douglas, who profoundly affected Old Testament scholarship, studied the relationship of purity, holiness, and creation. In her book *Purity and Danger*, she wrote: "Holiness means keeping distinct the categories of creation. It therefore involves correct definition, discrimination, and order. Under this head all the rules of sexual morality exemplify the holy."[26] Christine McCann commented on this: "By this definition, *anything which is against the natural order of things is necessarily unholy.*"[27] Scripturally, there is an intrinsic link between holiness and the created order.

Symbolized Holiness

Douglas's greatest contribution to Old Testament studies was her thesis that to understand the meaning of a cultic or ritual act, one had to first understand the overarching symbolic universe of a particular rite.[28] In other words, the part can only be understood in relation to the whole. The fundamental key to unpacking Hebraic culture is *holiness*.

The existence of Israel as God's people was, again, predicated on their status of holiness. In embracing a rebellious stance toward God (sin), man put himself into a sphere that was antithetical to God's holiness.

This had a fracturing effect and transformed man's experience of reality. Before sin, there was only the tangible nearness of God and the total transparency of relationships. This was the state of *shalom*, of integrated peace. After the Fall, man's condition is characterized by fear. From this point onward, man's reality becomes a world characterized by spheres of opposing forces.

In fact, Israel's cult was *primarily* concerned with enabling Israel to negotiate or avoid the spheres that were inimical to God. The role of the priests was "to distinguish between the holy and the common, and between the unclean and the clean" (Lev. 10:10). Whenever an Israelite became unclean (impure), he had to go through the prescribed ritual of purification at the appropriate time. For example, a woman having her menstrual cycle and producing blood or a man with leprous skin diseases or bodily discharges would become unclean or impure (Lev. 12–15). As their impure state conflicted with the holiness of God, they could not enter the sanctuary/temple. Their state was inimical to the holiness of God. The link connecting all the conditions (blood, disease, mold) that made one impure or unclean was that they were all connected to or symbolized death.

In paradise, man experienced the immediate presence of God, and he could do so because there was nothing in him that was antithetical to God's nature (i.e., his holiness). In the expulsion, the world once integrated by *shalom* is now fractured into conflicting states (the holy and common, pure and impure).[29] The covenant God makes with Moses provides a place (the temple) in the created order where the experience of Eden could be lived microcosmically. Here, the holiness of God existed palpably in the Holy of Holies. Death, which is contrary to God, who is life, comes about because of sin. Consequently, in order to enter the temple as one would enter Eden, one could not carry the vestiges of death (be in a state antithetical to holiness/life) or there would be a deadly confrontation.[30]

But holiness did not only exist in the temple. The *home* was seen as a little temple (*miskan katan*) and was also a sphere of holiness. This was emphasized even more after the temple was destroyed in A.D. 70. Using the work of noted rabbinic scholar Samuel Hirsch, Kaufman parallels the high priest's entering the divine presence at Yom Kippur with the preparation of the wife for the marital embrace. Both require the total immersion water ritual of *mikveh*:

> Hirsch compares the married woman's immersion in . . . waters of the *mikvah* prior to resuming marital relations to the *kohen's* [priest's] immersion in the *mikvah* prior to entering the sanctuary for the temple service in Jerusalem. On Yom Kippur, the climax of the Temple ritual was the entry of . . . the high priest, into . . . the Holy of Holies. Five times during the day, before each major service, he would immerse himself in a *mikvah*. The immersions were symbolic acts of purification which had the effect of raising his spiritual status.[31]

This view shows how in Judaism both the holiness of the conjugal union and the holiness of the encounter of God's people with God in the person of the high priest are ordered to each other and participate in the holiness of God. This coherence with, and participation in, the holiness of God is the key criterion for the evaluation of the marital embrace and any willed actions that interact with it.

Behavior and Holiness in Ancient Israel

Having seen that in ancient Israel human acts were evaluated in terms of their effect on the community's status of covenantal holiness, we can now examine two key texts. The first is the Onan incident in Genesis 38.

Judah had two sons, Er and Onan. Er was wicked and was killed by the Lord. According to the cultural custom of the time, Onan was supposed to have sexual relations with his brother's widow to continue his brother's family line. Onan, however, frustrated this obligation: "But Onan knew that the offspring would not be his; so when he went in to his brother's wife he spilled the semen on the ground" (Gen. 38:9).

Within both the Jewish and Christian communities, there has been a long and consistent tradition of seeing Onan's activity as a form of *coitus interruptus*. *Tractate Niddah* 13a, which is part of the record of rabbinical teachings called the *Talmud* (fourth to fifth century A.D.), states that "whosoever emits semen in vain deserves death, for it is said in Scripture, *And the thing which he did was evil in the sight of the Lord, and he slew him also . . . He is as though he shed blood.*"[32] This text interprets Onan's act of *wasting seed* as a mortal offense. Further, the text gives the reason for the gravity of the offence: *to waste seed is like committing murder.* This idea, well established in the rabbinical tradition, is based on the biblical idea of corporate personality, in which the family is understood as a single massive organic whole comprising, in a real sense, the past ancestors, the present generation, and the future posterity that will come.[33]

Another rabbinical text, *Yebamoth 34b*, states that "after a woman gives birth, her husband penetrates inside and spills his semen outside . . . so that his wife not become pregnant . . . These acts are nothing other than acts similar to those of Er and Onan, which are prohibited." In either case, the strict biblical prohibition against spilling seed was maintained. In Scripture and in Judaism, the constant teaching has always been that preventing semen from continuing in its procreative journey (whether it achieves this or not) is a grave sin.

Attempts to explain that Onan's death was not due to the act of wasting seed but rather resulted from his not being willing to carry out the levirate marriage—attempts that pave the way for challenging HV—are not convincing. The Mosaic Law would later stipulate *public shaming* as the punishment for refusing to carry out one's levirate duty (Deut. 25:9), not the death penalty. To warrant death, a graver sin was needed, and Genesis 38:9–10 links the punishment to the wasting or ruining of seed.[34]

Thus, according to Jewish law, two key biblical texts that provide parameters for the evaluation of sexual behavior are the commandment to be fruitful and multiply (Gen. 1:28) and the law against wasting (spoiling, killing) male seed (Gen. 38).[35] Underlying these condemnations of sexual behaviors that are against nature and its *telos*, and of actions that reject the capacity for the transmission of life within the sexual act, is the concern with holiness. To interfere with the unity of bodies ordered to their teleological end and willed by God in the order of creation is an offense against God's holiness of such magnitude as to deserve death.

III. The Christian Experience

For Christians, the advent of Christ is the decisive moment in human history, ushering in the final stage of man's salvation. A person's incorporation into Christ is of such ontological depths that he is described as "a new creation" (2 Cor. 5:17), indicating both a radical continuity and a radical discontinuity with all that had gone on before. In the Sermon on the Mount, Jesus revealed his work to be one of fulfillment. He said, "Think not that I have come to abolish the law and the prophets; I have come not to abolish them but to fulfill them."

Jesus indicates that fulfillment functions as a before/after marker. "For truly, I say to you . . . not an iota, not a dot, will pass from the law *until* all is accomplished." Thus, nothing changes until the law is fulfilled, *but once accomplished*, the transformation of God's covenantal relationship with us and with creation becomes possible.

Jesus provides examples of what a radicalized and interiorized understanding of the law looks like:

> "You have heard that it was said to the men of old, `You shall not kill . . . But I say to you that everyone who is angry with his brother shall be liable to judgment" (Matt. 5:21–22a).

> "You have heard that it was said, 'You shall not commit adultery.' But I say to you that everyone who looks at a woman lustfully has already committed adultery with her in his heart" (Matt. 5:27–28).

Jesus' teachings reveal the underlying *logos* of the law. He teaches that the righteousness of the observant Pharisees was not sufficient for salvation (Matt. 5:20). They certainly read Moses and "knew" the law, but it was clear they did not grasp its interiority, which the Logos himself was now showing them. The context of the Sermon on the Mount provides the textual clue for the source of this radical authority. Forging a typological link, Jesus goes up the mountain and takes on the role of the new Moses. He authoritatively re-describes the law, revealing that salvific righteousness flows from living in union with the logos of the Torah (its interior truth) and not an exterior obedience. As Paul teaches, the law was good, but it was not enough. It served not to effect salvation (which it could not do) but to enable man to realize the depth of his separation from God's holiness (cf. Gal. 3:23–24).

This level of transformation is now possible for two reasons. First, Jesus is the intelligibility of all things, through whom all things come into existence (John 1:1–3). Second, Jesus came to effect a radical change in the order of creation; he is overcoming the effects of the Fall.

> He said to them, "For by your hardness of heart Moses allowed you to divorce your wives, but from the beginning it was not so. And I say to you: whoever divorces his wife, except for unchastity, and marries another, commits adultery" (Matt. 19:8).

Divorce was an accepted reality within Judaism. Therefore, in calling divorce and remarriage adultery, Jesus is proclaiming something radically new; creation is being restored *to its original intentionality*. The distorting power of the Fall has effectively been healed and a new way of living now obtains. "What therefore God has joined together, let man not separate" (Matt. 19:6). The old order (exemplified by the hardness of heart) has passed away and a new order in creation (concretized in the indissolubility of the one-flesh union) is emerging. God restores and secures the indissolubility of the male-female union through the cross. To bring division or separation into this profound, divinely willed union of bodies is to reject the salvific work of Christ.

Apprehending the truth is not always straightforward. Initially, the disciples did not understand how Jesus' teaching could be possible. They were scandalized and said, "If such is the case of a man with his wife, it is not expedient to marry" (Matt 19:10). Even for the chosen disciples, the truths of Christ's kingdom were not always easy to understand. To receive (have docility toward) and apprehend (understand the meaning of) these truths would require a process initiated and guided by the Holy Spirit. As Jesus had taught his disciples: "I have many more things to say to you, but you cannot bear them now. But when the Spirit of truth, comes, he will guide you into all the truth" (John 16:12–13).

Paul's Appropriation of the Law

In his own personal history, Paul gives an example of Jesus' transformative effect on the order of creation. Paul was a Pharisee of the Pharisees and had sat at the feet of Gamaliel, one of the most famous rabbis of that era (Phil. 3:1–8; Acts 23:3). Paul would have had an authoritative command of both Scripture and rabbinical teaching, including those texts dealing with sexual purity. Paul's adherence to the law led him to hunt down and have killed Christians whom he saw as heretical Jews. But around A.D. 34, Paul experienced the risen Christ (Acts 9). All the categories of his mind were shaken.

Once Paul saw Jesus as the fulfillment of the law, he had to reevaluate all he had learned and, interestingly, grounds his anthropology directly on the biblical witness. Through Christ, the risen Logos, Paul begins to see the inner theological meaning of creation and the one-flesh union. Creation becomes a critical category. In Romans, Paul begins his theological argument concerning sin by grounding it in creation. This passage has played a key role in the formation of the Christian moral sense, so it will be quoted at length:

> For what can be known about God is plain to them [the wicked], because God has shown it to them . . . his invisible nature . . . has been clearly perceived in the things

that have been made. So they are without excuse; for although they knew God they did not honor him as God
. . . and their senseless minds were darkened . . . Therefore God gave them . . . to impurity, to the dishonoring
of their bodies among themselves, *because they exchanged
the truth about God for a lie* . . . For this reason God gave
them up to dishonorable passions. Though they know
God's decree that those who do such things deserve to
die, they not only do them but approve those who practice them (Rom. 1:19–32, emphasis added).

For Paul, creation reflects the nature of God. That is, the
physical reality of things is encoded with the truth of God
and, hence, is reflective of his being. *Paul then ties the rejection
of God to immoral behavior.* As he develops his theme, the iconic
form the rebellion against God takes is perverting the natural
use of the body. Paul writes, "Their women exchanged natural relations for unnatural, and the men likewise gave up natural relations with women and were consumed with passion
for one another" (Rom. 1:26–27). For Paul, to reject God's
intentionality is to reject God, and ends up in various forms of
immorality, especially the misuse of the sexual function of the
body. This is the "lie" that fallen man has accepted.[36]

Here, in the light of Christ, Paul is deepening the Old
Testament understanding of what offends God's order and
holiness. In the Old Testament, only male homosexual practices were condemned with the death penalty (Lev. 18:22,
20:13) since only these wasted male seed. But Paul expands
the Old Testament and rabbinical perspective to recognize
that both male and female homosexual practices are against
God's original design for the human person.

Paul's theology is grounded in the new creation in Christ
(2 Cor. 5:17) and a radical understanding of the body's

functioning in the salvifically restored order of creation. In it we find a number of important criteria for seeing if behaviors cohere with or reject the holiness of God.

1. Integral Unity of Body and Soul

Genesis 2:7 shows that man is a composite unity of body and soul.[37] There can be no dualistic approach to man, as his body and spirit function as a unity. In Hebrew thought, man does not have a soul, he *is* a soul, which means that in human actions, both body and soul interpenetrate each other, forming one reality. Therefore, willed acts of the body affect the spiritual life and capacity of the person. In assuming a human nature, Jesus raises the dignity of the human body. *God is forevermore united to human flesh, showing that flesh can cohere with the holiness of God.*

2. The Significance of Bodily Acts

It was Jesus' acts in history that effected man's salvation. Contrary to any gnostic beliefs,[38] and specifically in addressing ideas of a non-bodily salvation, Paul consistently shows that immoral bodily acts contradict the holiness Christians are called to and thus separate them from Christ. In Romans 6, Paul addresses this issue and asks, "How can we who died to sin [in Christ, in baptism] still live in it" (v.2). One's whole being must be oriented to God and his holiness.

3. Following the Way of the Cross

Colossians 1:24 articulates the Pauline doctrine of cooperation: "Now I rejoice in my sufferings for your sake, and in my flesh I complete what is lacking in Christ's afflictions for the sake of his body, that is, the church." Christians are called to participate in the sufferings of Christ. By letting go of the ego and surrendering it to Christ, we follow him on his path of redemptive suffering. Rather than asserting our own will, we freely renounce our claims, limiting ourselves, opening ourselves to frustration and pain as a way of furthering the work of Christ. Ironically, it is the denial of self (our desires, passions, and our drives) and not self-fulfillment that leads to eternal life. As Paul writes to the Galatians: "Those who belong to Christ Jesus have crucified the flesh with its passions and desires" (5:24).

4. Cooperation with Grace

For Paul, salvation is a *both/and* process. The initial act that justifies man can only come from the outside of man via the passion and death of Our Lord. But once the right ordering (i.e., justification) has been restored, the gift of salvation has to be worked out, in and through the bodily acts of the human person.

In Philippians, Paul shows the dual aspect of salvation. He commands the Philippians to "work out your own salvation with fear and trembling; for God is at work in you, both to will and to work for his good pleasure" (Phil. 2:12–13). First, the human person is called to active participation as he "works out" his salvation, which only God can procure (Rom. 5:8–9). But God is *already* at work in the person, giving the grace needed to work out this gift. Salvation—the coherence of man with God's holiness—is initiated by grace, continues in grace, and is finally accomplished by grace, but it also requires man's cooperation.

5. The Indwelling Spirit

As St. John came to understand the deeper dimensions of the Logos working in creation, so Paul also came to understand the deeper dimension of the cross in the created order and the relationship of the human body to the process of salvation.

Christ breathed upon his disciples to receive the Holy Spirit, the Spirit of truth. This Spirit was to lead the Church "into all truth" (John 16:13). What was only partially glimpsed by the old covenant is now more fully known.

This *Spirit-led* knowledge enabled Paul and the Church to understand that a) the call to holiness is written within the whole of human bodily existence, b) human acts either cooperate with or act against our nature given by God in creation, and c) these acts either move us toward or away from communion with the holiness of God. Paul, led further by the Logos, goes deeper into the mystery of man and is shown that d) one-flesh union *and* the fruitfulness to which it is ordered are bound together as an iconic expression of Christ's inseparable union with the Church, and e) marital union is grounded in and derives its meaning from the relationship of Christ with the Church. This is the revealing of the final theological form of marriage.

6. The Nuptial Theme of Salvation

Within Hebrew revelation, the *nuptial* understanding of Yahweh's relationship with Israel grew denser, particularly in the prophets where Yahweh is described as the husband of his people (Hos. 1–3; Isa. 54:5). In Hosea, the Lord says, "I will betroth you to me forever; I will betroth you to me in righteousness and . . . steadfast love" (2:16–20). These nuptials are fulfilled when John the Baptist announces that the Bridegroom had come (John 3:29). But there is no explicit development of this theme until we come to Paul's epistles, where it becomes a foundational theological concept.

Paul writes to the Corinthians, "I betrothed you to Christ to present you as a pure bride to her one husband" (1 Cor. 11:2). The apex of this nuptial theme is given in Ephesians. Here the *novum* of Christ, in regard to marriage, is announced for the first time. The presentation uniquely emphasizes the sacrificial and cultic dimensions of the one-flesh unity, as well as the purity, holiness, and convertibility of these two realities.

Temple Imagery and Sacrificial Language

The central theme of Ephesians is "unity" and it is expressed in the word *anakephalaiōsasthai*, ("to gather together under one head"):

> The mystery of his will . . . a plan for the fullness of time, to unite [*anakephalaiōsasthai*], all things in him [Christ], things in heaven and things on earth (Eph. 1:9–10).

Later, Paul says "there is one body and one Spirit . . . one hope . . . one Lord, one faith, one baptism, one God and Father of us all" (Eph. 4:4–6). Toward the end of the letter, Paul takes up the final unity of the marital embrace and identifies this with the unity of Christ and the Church: "This is a great mystery, but I am speaking about Christ and the Church" (Eph. 5:22–32). In 5:1, Paul asks the Ephesians to become "imitators of Christ," and when he comprehensively applies this to marital relations in 5:22–32, he uses that opportunity to articulate a *new theological norm* that constitutes the real form of marriage. This norm provides the framework for moral evaluation of *willed behaviors extrinsically inserted into the one-flesh union* of man and woman. In a sudden moment of insight, Paul presents the essential reciprocity or convertibility of the man-woman relationship with the Christ-Church relationship (Eph. 5:32).

This passage underscores the organic *unity* of the couple that functions as an integrated whole. As von Balthasar notes, Paul "does not mean here that the two partners, as individual

Christians, must each follow Christ, he makes it very clear that their marriage itself is to be a reflection of the relationship between Christ and the Church."[39] Here the theme of unity in the letter reaches its culmination: one Lord, one faith, one God and Father, the one-flesh union of man and woman intersecting with the oneness of Christ and the Church.[40]

Critically, Paul presents the Christ-Church nexus as the archetype of human marriage. He says that the husband is the head of the wife, *as* Christ is the head of the Church" (5:23). The husband is to love his wife *as* "Christ loved the Church, and gave himself for her" (5:25). Thus, in an unprecedented unveiling, Paul discloses that human marital communion is fulfilled when it takes on its ecclesial identity, an identity that is not arbitrary but willed by God to participate in and show the drama of his redemptive love.

At the core of the union of man and woman is an *imitatio Christi*: Christ-like humility (submission) and Christ-like sacrifice (laying down one's life). The cultic language is explicitly developed in verses 5:26–27. Christ sanctifies the Church, cleanses her, so that she does not have a spot. The result is that the Church will be without blemish and is to be holy. These terms relate to the temple sacrificial cult where *purity* was essential to holiness. In like manner, men are to love their wives in imitation of Christ.

Thus, for Paul, purity, sacrifice, purification and holiness are not Old Testament categories that have been overcome, but rather are *fulfilled* in Christ and lived out in human marriage which functions as a *participatory icon*. Marriage becomes a holy offering to God *through* the mutual sacrificial offering of the spouses. Human acts in marriage are grounded in the salvific process and are a representation of the salvific acts of Christ. Any action contrary to this sacrificial offering, which always opens up to life, would be antithetical to the meaning of the one-flesh union of man and woman as well as the union between Christ and the Church.

In 5:28–32, Paul reveals that the sacrifice of Christ is the ground of marriage. Paul's claim is that Christ's loving his body, the Church, penetrates the reality of a man's loving his wife as his own body. The ontological bond between Christ and his body is somehow reflected in the one-flesh union of man and woman. They both are single, integrated psycho-somatic organisms. At this point, he refers to both human and divine unions as a "great mystery." Paul is not drawing an analogy here; rather he posits a reciprocal equivalence between the two forms of union.[41] Scripture scholar André Villeneuve writes about this imitation of Christ: "This is the type of sacrificial love that husbands should imitate for the sake of their brides. It would presumably involve a long and arduous process of "practicing death" in self-denial, self-mortification and kenosis (self-emptying) in imitation of Christ."[42]

If this were mere analogy, it would give no help in our quest to develop biblical criteria by which to evaluate contraceptive behavior affecting the martial embrace. If, on the other hand, there is an ontological link between Christian marriage and Christ-Church spirituality, then the question becomes whether or not contraceptive behavior enables or hinders the practice of humility, self-denial, and the bearing of one's cross—that is, the spiritual and iconic reality of the one-flesh union.

Thus, the New Testament as led by the Logos has enabled God's community to understand at ever greater levels:

a) the order of creation and how it is tied to the Logos and therefore proclaims the will of God,
b) the broader application of what acts against nature interiorly mean,

c) the direct link to rebellion against God and the rejection of the teleological purpose of the functions of the human body in sexual acts, and

d) the final revelation of the theological form of marriage, which intrinsically unites the act of Christ on the cross and the union of man and woman, such that both are caught up in the salvific activity of God and concretize his holiness.

Understanding these things, we see how anything that eviscerates the God-designed capacity for procreation in the one-flesh union acts against the order of creation, which in Christ can no longer remain mute. Anything that interferes with the unitive aspect of the conjugal embrace (whether physically or spiritually) ultimately attacks the power and capacity of the sexual union to image and carry the salvific love of Christ and to incarnate that love in the world.

Back to the Zygote Paradigm

We started this chapter by showing that sacred texts need the God-given mechanism of interpretation in order to secure revelational truth that is binding. In this light we now ask, how has the community of God's people understood these texts and what, if any, binding teaching have they proposed from them?

What we find is a unanimous and unified understanding and teaching over the millennia, with no deviation. From the early Church onward, the act of Onan was seen as a form of self-abuse directly against the order of nature (by depriving human seed of its God-given end), as well as against the lives of future persons. Such acts were clearly incompatible with God's holiness and were considered grave sin.

The Patristic witness bears this out. The first-century *Letter of Barnabas* condemns oral sex as immoral.[43] St. Clement of Alexandria (A.D. 190–215) links sexual activity with procreation and the natural order: "To indulge in intercourse without intending children is to outrage nature, whom we should take as our instructor."[44] Hippolytus (170–236) denounces women who "began to resort to drugs for producing sterility"[45] Epiphanius (315–403) writes about "those who when they have intercourse deliberately prevent having children they betray the work of God by perverting it to their own deceits.[46]

St. Jerome (347–420) in *Letter to Eustochium* portrays contraception as a form of murder: "Others drink potions to ensure sterility and are guilty of murdering a human being not yet conceived."[47] St. John Chrysostom (349–407) condemns those who "maimed their nature not only by slaying their children after birth, but not even agreeing to conceive.[48] St. Caesarius of Arles (470–542) writes, "They have committed as many murders as the number of the children they might have begotten."[49] And St. Augustine (354–430) synthesizes the Church's teaching concerning the transmission of life:

> The institution of marriage exists for the sake of generation . . . There are some lawfully wedded couples . . . intercourse . . . can take place in an unlawful and shameful manner, whenever the conception of offspring is avoided. Onan, the son of Juda, did this very thing, and the Lord slew him on that account. Therefore, the procreation of children is itself the primary, natural, legitimate purpose of marriage.[50]

These texts show the consistent thinking of the Church, based on the order of creation (illustrated in Genesis 38), that sexual activity does not exist as an autonomous good and can never be separated from the good of procreation. Thus, the willed blocking of conception within the marital act was always seen as grave, against nature, and even a form of murder. This became codified in the *Decretals of Burchard* (c. 1000), which stated: "If someone, to satisfy his lust or in deliberate hatred does something to a man or woman so that no child be born of him or her, or gives them to drink, so that he cannot generate or she conceive, let it be held as homicide."[51] John T. Noonan found the same understanding in the Penitential Books from 500–1000.[52]

This understanding held even in Protestantism after the Reformation, until the twentieth century. Both Luther and Calvin maintained the Jewish-Catholic teaching on sexual union and contraceptive behavior. Luther wrote:

> This is a most disgraceful sin. This far more atrocious than incest and adultery. We call it unchastity, yes, a Sodomitic sin. For Onan goes into her; that is, lies with her and copulates, and when it comes to the point of insemination, spills the seed, lest the woman conceive. Surely at such a time the order of nature established by God in procreation should be followed."[53]

Calvin's assessment was even stronger:

> It is a horrible thing to pour out seed besides the intercourse of man and woman. Deliberately avoiding the intercourse, so that the seed drops on the ground, is double horrible. For this . . . kills the son . . . before he is born.[54]

This unanimous condemnation of contraceptive behavior held until 1930 with the notorious Lambeth Conference's acceptance of contraception. Pope Pius XI wrote *Casti Connubii* in direct response to the Anglican Communion's official legitimization of contraceptive behavior. The encyclical presented the constant Catholic (as well as Protestant) teaching on this subject, referencing Onan and Augustine's understanding of that incident.

> But no reason, however grave, may be put forward by which anything intrinsically against nature may become conformable to nature and morally good. Since, therefore, the conjugal act is destined primarily by nature for the begetting of children, those who in exercising it *deliberately frustrate its natural power and purpose* sin against nature and commit a deed which is shameful and intrinsically vicious (*Casti Connubi* 54).

Following the zygote model we mentioned earlier, here (and ultimately with HV) we have the raw DNA data[55] and the reception and interpretation of this information by its God-given interpretative matrix (the Church) yielding a unanimous and consistent understanding of the human person and the purpose of the sexual act. Through centuries of organic interaction between the two, there has been continuous deepening of the understanding of the holiness of sexual union and a more-precise identification of what works against its meaning, function, and holiness in the created order.

How do we apply all this as we enter *Humanae Vitae's* fifty-first year and beyond?

The authoritative witness of Scripture and the Church on contraceptive acts is uniform, comprehensive, and unanimous.

According to that witness, creation has never been considered a neutral piece of data over which we exercise control. (That is the attitude of technology, which underlies much of modern thinking.[56]) Rather, creation means, first and foremost, that there is a Creator whom we are called to worship and obey.

These are difficult terms for our modern society to accept, with its emphasis on human freedom. Nevertheless, to obey means to accept and work within the nature that the Creator has given us. Our nature, as sexually differentiated, is ordered to another with whom we form a one-flesh unity that is also ordered simultaneously, *by its given nature,* to both communion and procreation. The privileged expression of this personal communion is achieved through the genital members of the body, whose teleological purpose is procreative. In the use of these members, genetic material is produced which has no other purpose than the continuation of the human race. By their God-given design and nature, these two functions are inseparable. Man's dual unity of body and spirit is concretized in this sexual act, ordered to both communion and new life. To separate body and soul causes the death of the body; when we separate the marital embrace's meanings of communion and life, it produces another form of death.

Beyond the physical level, human sexuality also participates in and manifests the inner communion and life of God. Ultimately, the one-flesh union of man is a reflective and iconic participation in Christ's love for the Church. The human sexual embrace, with its openness to communion and new life is grounded and participates in the Christ-Church love. If this is more than metaphor, then what we do in the one relationship affects the other. Therefore, to use contraception to annihilate the ability to have life within the context of communion in marriage gravely harms the foundation of our salvific relationship with Christ.

We have entertained a long theological amnesia about the pedagogical value of a divinely willed creation. Our emphasis on the human subjective experience, coupled with the value of human freedom, has sometimes caused us to mute the voice of creation. We have distanced ourselves from the Onan incident as a contraceptive act even though Scripture and rabbinical writings witness to this act specifically as a form of contraception—an understanding that has been taught constantly in the Church's history. Creation shows (and the Onan incident makes clear) that there is an integrity to the act of sexual communion that begins a process, the structure of which man has no authority to pervert, and that must always be respected and must be allowed its full development once begun. *Humanae Vitae* takes this into full account when it condemns "every action which, either in anticipation of the conjugal act, or in its accomplishment, or in the development of its natural consequences, proposes, whether as an end or as a means, to render procreation impossible" (14).

The fundamental revelation that has been bequeathed to the Church is the nature of the "great mystery" of marriage. The subtext embedded in Genesis 2 showing the covenantal nature of marriage becomes fully revealed on the cross, where Christ as the Bridegroom gives his life for his beloved Bride, the Church. This is the prototype for all marriages and is fully realized in sacramental marriage. Paul shows us that the one-flesh sexual union of man and woman participates in the holiness of Christ's total self-offering for, and his union with, his Bride.

The cultic language of Ephesians 5 shows us that the union of man and woman is more than a physical reality. It truly is *sacramental*. It brings us into an encounter with the living God. Like the high priest entering the Holy of the

Holies, to honor God and to fulfill his intention we need to be in a state of holiness in our martial embrace. Therefore, there can be nothing in the structure of the act that is antithetical to God or his holiness. But preventing the full and complete union of man and woman or the processes that God has willed as part of that union is antithetical to God and his holiness, because it is an attempt to become the author of life ourselves—falsifying our relationship to the Creator, falsifying the meaning of our bodies, and making that act unholy. As with ancient Israel, God calls us to be holy with and in our bodily acts. If we refuse, we cannot enjoy communion with him.

Paul's revelation was that God created the one-flesh union (expressed in the sexual union of man and woman) as an earthly expression of the unity and communion of his own inner life and as a participating icon of Christ's love for the Church. Contraception attacks this theological form of marriage. The *telos* of the body (ordered to an indissoluble unity of communion and life reflecting the inner life of God and the cross) is rejected and one meaning is annihilated in a misguided attempt to enhance the other, preventing the act's iconic participation in the unity within God and the unity of Christ and the Church. We reject God (and his truth of indissoluble unity) for the lie of isolated pleasure. Theologically, we attack the indivisible unity of the divine Trinitarian life that gendered sexual union is meant to express.

Finally, contraception, which wills to separate the transmission of life from sexual union, reduces conjugal love to an experience without a form. The body appears to function in the manner for which it was created, the pleasure of communion appears to be achieved, but when the *telos* of the body and the full union are removed from the act, then even those appearances have been falsified and are emptied of their integral meaning.

Referring to the indissolubility of marriage, Jesus warned us not to separate what God has joined together (Matt. 19). Likewise, Scripture teaches that in the sexual act the mutually informing meanings of *life* inscribed within *communion* must never be separated or they will perish. What God has joined together, let not man separate.

~

2

The Meaning and Purpose of Human Sexuality

Paul Gondreau

It was about three o'clock in the afternoon on July 5, 1902, when a young Italian girl found herself fending off the sexual advances of her nineteen-year-old neighbor. Crying, "No, it is a sin! God does not want it!" the girl did succeed in thwarting the rape, but at the cost of her life.

Exacerbated by the girl's elusiveness and succumbing to his rage, the young man began to choke the girl, and after she asserted that she would rather die than submit, he proceeded to stab her repeatedly. She survived, but only for a few hours. Approximately twenty hours after the assault, the young girl, clutching a cross to her chest and gazing upon a picture of the Blessed Mother, surrendered her last breath, but not before forgiving her assailant and praying that he would be with her in heaven.

Forty-eight years later, Pope Pius XII, recognizing the need for the witness of a young girl who prized her chastity and purity above her own life, added this young girl's name,

Maria Goretti, to the list of canonized saints and martyrs of the universal Church. Half a million pilgrims attended the canonization, including Alessandro Serenelli, her murderer, who stood alongside Maria's mother, Assunta. Initially unrepentant, three years into his prison sentence Alessandro had been visited by Maria in a dream in which she offered him lilies, a traditional image of virginity. He began to pray to her, and after his release from prison, he became a Capuchin lay brother, living and working in a monastery as a gardener until his death in 1970.

"A New and Utterly Perverse Morality"

Pope Pius XII was eager to canonize Maria Goretti, patron saint of chastity and purity, because, as he proclaimed at her canonization, she provides us with a "Saint Agnes of the twentieth century"—that is, with someone who can help youths in their need to "resist attacks on their chastity." (Tradition records that the young Roman maiden Agnes, after rebuffing the advances of a Roman praetor's son, found herself exposed in the Stadium of Domitian—the present Piazza Navona in Rome—but had her purity and modesty preserved by a miraculous growth of hair that covered her nakedness; in the end, though, she was martyred by beheading.) Faced with what his predecessor, Pope Pius XI, had decried in *Casti Connubii* as "a new and utterly perverse morality" and "the power of unbridled lust," Pius XII knew well how dire this need was.

Yet scarcely could this same pontiff, who himself had bemoaned the loss of a sense of sin as the chief offense of the twentieth century, have predicted the near total collapse of sexual morals, nowhere more poignantly seen than in the war on procreation that technological advances in contraception occasioned merely half a century later. Already by 1968, of course, Pope Paul VI spied the need to intervene. As we now know, his intervention triggered an earthquake in the Church, the aftershocks of which extend to our very day. Famously deciding against the recommendation of his own papal commission,[57] in *Humanae Vitae* (HV) Paul VI opted to follow the opinion of the minority group of advisors, including the little-known Polish cardinal Karol Wojtyla (the future John Paul II), and renewed the Church's traditional condemnation of the use of contraceptives.[58] He went further, warning that widespread contraceptive use would lead to an increase in marital infidelity, the objectification of women by men ("a mere instrument for the satisfaction of his own desire"), the coercive use of birth control by governments, and "a general lowering of moral standards" (17).

As we know only too well, Paul VI's warnings went unheeded, and we now find ourselves facing a full frontal assault on the meaning and purpose of human sexuality.

"Turned to Madness and Evil"

Pius XI may have decried the "new and utterly perverse morality" of the early 1930s, but we can wonder whether in his worst nightmares he could have imagined how less than a century later Western societies would toss sex wholly to the winds of moral relativism and how irrepressible hedonism would be spawned by the notion of autonomy as freedom from external influence (whether that influence comes from nature, God, or the Church).

Could he have foreseen, for instance, Western nations at risk of contracepting and aborting themselves out of existence? Or, worse, could he have foreseen state governments declaring same-sex unions to be identical in kind to heterosexual unions—to the point most recently of prominent churchmen, cardinals even, voicing their desire to explore ways for the Church to "bless" homoerotic unions—thereby relegating the order of nature to the waste bin of irrelevance?

Could he have foreseen the growing cultural accommodation, ever increasingly through legal coercion, of the view that one's biological sex remains alien to one's sexual self-identity ("gender"), with the result that individuals (even children) now have the "right" not only to identify themselves as "transgender," "genderqueer," "agender," "bigender," "third gender," "gender-fluid" (and so on—the options are endless), but also a right to the medical therapies, surgeries, and bodily mutilations deemed necessary to affirm those identities?

Could he have foreseen still other high-ranking churchmen speaking of a "paradigm shift" in the Church's moral teaching, particularly as it concerns adultery (or what used to be considered adultery) in the case of divorced and civilly remarried Catholics? And we have barely scratched the surface of egregious examples. "Turned to madness and evil" seems as apt a description of today's social regard for sexual choices and lifestyles as when J.R.R. Tolkien has Gandalf the wizard say it of Lord Denethor in *The Lord of the Rings* after Denethor had lost his mind and ordered his own death and the death of his innocent son.

To be sure, seeing this turn toward "madness and evil" as marking an unprecedented moment in human history, in his 2012 year-end address to the Roman Curia Pope Benedict XVI pointed out that a "new philosophy of sexuality" has taken hold of Western culture.[59] By this he meant the view that sees sex "no longer [as] a given element of nature," but instead as "a social role that we choose for ourselves." He went further, adding that the current crisis facing the "true structure of the family, made up of father, mother, and child" calls into question "the very notion of what being human really means." Here Benedict was amplifying his message for the World Day of Peace that he had issued a week earlier, wherein he reiterated what Catholic moral teaching has always professed about "the natural structure of marriage as the union of a man and a woman," namely, that it is "inscribed in human nature itself, accessible to reason and thus common to all humanity."[60]

What Does It Mean to Be Human?

With this, Benedict places us at the heart of the problem, indeed, at the heart of the teaching of *Humanae Vitae*. More than a dispute over contraception, the controversy stirred by HV (and more generally the current dispute over sexual choices and lifestyles) is at bottom a dispute over what it means to be human. *Humanae Vitae* itself implies as much when it places at the core of its teaching "the inseparable connection, established by God, which man on his own initiative may not break, between the unitive significance and the procreative significance which are both inherent in the marital act" (12). For what prompts this affirmation of the inseparable connection between procreation and unitive love, I submit, is a view of the human being as a *body-soul unity*. Where one stands on the fundamental structure of our *human nature* determines where one stands on HV, and, more generally, on the meaning and purpose of our sexuality.

Put in other terms, one's position on the moral quality of sexual action, whether one realizes it or not, is necessarily predicated on a deeper anthropology. What the prevalence of procreative-free sex exposes, then—as Benedict well perceived—is a deeply problematic view of human nature that today's "new philosophy of sexuality" harbors. Lurking behind the dispute over the meaning and purpose of our sexuality, as behind the dispute over HV, lies a distorted anthropology.

The upshot is clear: at stake in the dispute over sexual sin (contraception included) is nothing less than the truth of the human person. Such high stakes help explain why we see, on the one side, secular culture seeking ever aggressively, by calumny and ridicule, to rope the Church into the arena of odium, and, on the other, the Church remaining steadfast in defending the true meaning and purpose of human sexuality. The Church must ever "safeguard marriage [as a procreative-unitive institution], as much as possible, from error and violence and deceit," as Pope Leo XIII put it back in 1880 (*Arcanum* 15), just as the Church must ever safeguard the truth of the human person.

So, yes, HV remains as controversial as ever. Some observers think the encyclical has inflicted "major damage" on the Church, and they bemoan the fact that the Church speaks "'too much' about the sixth commandment and sin."[61] But speak out on the "sixth commandment" (not simply adultery, but more generally the proper moral use of our sexuality) the Church must, since at bottom the Church is speaking out on the truth of the human person.

The Philosophy of the Body

In what follows we shall endeavor, after offering a cursory walk-through of the rival views of human nature, to flesh out the way Paul VI, in upholding the inseparable connection between the procreative and unitive aspects of marital love, was indeed naming the essential meaning and purpose of human sexuality. Observing the method of HV, whereby its teaching draws from both the light of human reason (what Benedict means by "accessible to reason and thus common to all humanity") and the light of divine revelation, I shall pursue this line of argument along both philosophical and theological grounds, though with greater focus on the first.

I shall end with a brief consideration of the implication this bears on those sexual practices that, in one way or another, violate the procreative and/or unitive purposes of sex.

A short word on articulating a vision of human sexuality by appealing to the authority of human reason—what we might call explicating a "philosophy of the body"—is in order. As indicated by Paul VI's addressing HV not simply to all Catholics, but "to all men of good will," the yield of such an endeavor is vast. It allows the Church—usually via appeal to the natural law—to cast the widest net possible and to direct its moral instruction to the human family as such ("all men of good will"). The Church's vision of human sexuality, though certainly employing rightly its authority with regard to divine revelation, is not exclusively faith-based, not exclusively a "Catholic thing." It is a "human" thing, accessible and applicable to all members of the human family, regardless of religious adherence (or lack thereof). This likens the Church's opposition to various sexual practices to its opposition, say, to rape, or arson, or murder, or theft, which any conscientious person, Catholic or not, will also oppose.

No one appreciated this more than John Paul II, who placed the natural law at the center of his great moral encyclical *Veritatis Splendor,* and Benedict XVI, tireless champion of appealing to the common moral fabric of our humanity. Consider, for instance, how the latter made this appeal in practically every one of his high-profile state visits: he reminded Americans in his 2008 apostolic visit that the Declaration of Independence expressly grounds in the natural law the inalienable rights to life, liberty, and the pursuit of happiness; he instructed the United Nations General Assembly in the same year that only the natural law could rescue the notion of human rights from the tyranny of moral relativism; in his address to the British Parliament in 2010, he cited the natural law as the proper source for objective moral norms; and in 2011 he disabused the German Bundestag of the view that natural law marks a "specifically Catholic doctrine" rather than a law that is accessible to human reason.

Benedict's assertion, then, that the meaning and purpose of human sexuality is "accessible to reason and thus common to all humanity" fits squarely with a chief aim of his pontificate, as with one of the principal thrusts not only of HV, but of the entire Catholic moral tradition, beginning with the apostle Paul himself (see Rom. 2:14–15).

One further introductory remark. Because HV draws upon the foundational principles of sexual action as expressive of the truth of our fundamental humanity, its teaching allows for practical application not simply in the area of birth regulation, but to all sexual practices. Enunciating foundational principles that extend to issues beyond what the encyclical sets out specifically to address, *Humanae Vitae*—we need unabashedly to declare it now fifty years later and should never tire of saying it—marks a great gift to the Church and to humanity. As Mary Eberstadt arrestingly puts the matter, "The most globally reviled and widely misunderstood document of the last half century is also the most prophetic and explanatory of our time."[62]

I. Rival Anthropologies

An Integrated View of the Human Being

Painting in broad strokes, we can say the clash of anthropologies mentioned above, and the subsequent clash of moral visions, boils down to two vastly divergent ways of viewing the role of the human body, inclusive of its biological hardwiring, in our human identity. On the one side (the Catholic side, the side of HV), we find what we can term an *integrated anthropology.* This anthropology identifies the human being as a body-soul unity, wherein the individual is as much identified with his body as with his soul. Though body and soul, the human being is paradoxically yet one.

According to this integrated anthropology, the body shares in the dignity and moral responsibility of one's personal identity. No one affirmed this in more thunderous fashion than St. Paul. Holding in mind the fact that "the immoral man sins against his own body," the apostle charges us to "glorify God in (our) body," as the body "is the temple of the Holy Spirit" (1 Cor. 6:18–20). "Radiance of the flesh" is how Dante's great medieval poem *The Divine Comedy* expresses the exalted view that this anthropology accords the human body; specifically, it comes in Dante's discussion of the final resurrection, when our souls shall be "robed about" in our glorified risen bodies, thereby making our humanity "lovelier for being whole."[63] No mere husk or shell, the human body, on Dante's account, is a glorious royal "robe" for the human soul. Without the body, the human person (Dante was thinking of the separated soul awaiting the final resurrection) remains incomplete. Human beings are not angels, not free-floating disembodied spirits that happened to be attached to material bodies.

In the Church's common tradition, the most ardent proponent of an integrated anthropology is St. Thomas Aquinas. Aquinas stands out on this score because he fuses a robust Aristotelian view that all things (save God and the angels) are composed of matter and form (or material "stuff" arranged or specified, via the form, into particular kinds of things) with the biblical account of creation, especially Genesis 2:7 ("then the Lord God formed man of dust from the ground, and breathed into his nostrils the breath of life; and man became a living being"). On Aquinas' account, the human being is a unified composite of organic matter that he shares with all other animals, and a rational form or soul that is unique to him. That is, what constitutes the human person is an animal body ("dust from the ground") and an immaterial or spiritual soul ("the breath of life"). Underscoring the nobility that such an account accords the body, and aware that matter (or body) is for the sake of form (or soul), Aquinas in one magnificent passage asserts that the human body, because of its dignity of being fitted for a rational soul, stands apart from all other bodies as the most excellent expression "of the divine art" *(ab arte divina).*[64] For Aquinas, the human body marks God's artistic masterpiece!

The Church continues to promote this integrated, body-soul view of the human being. The *Catechism,* for instance, citing the Council of Vienne (1311–12), affirms: "The unity of soul and body is so profound that one has to consider the soul to be the 'form' of the body . . . Spirit and matter, in man, are not two natures united, but rather their union forms a single nature" (365). John Paul II, who in *Fides et Ratio* insists that a "sound philosophical vision of human nature" must underpin any moral theology worthy of its name (68), made the human person's body-soul unity the cornerstone of his much-celebrated catechetical discourses on the "theology of the body." And at the centerpiece of his inaugural encyclical letter *Deus Caritas Est,* Benedict XVI places this same integrated view of the human person: "[I]t is neither the spirit alone nor the body alone that loves: it is man, the person, a unified creature composed of body and soul, who loves" (5).

A Fragmented Anthropology

Opposed to this integrated anthropology is an anthropology that can be termed *Cartesianist* (named after the seventeenth-century philosopher René Descartes), though some call it by other names, like *gnostic* or *angelistic*. Whatever the name, the reality remains the same: an anthropology that defines the human being not as a body-soul unity but as an autonomous thinking-choosing "self" who is only loosely or accidentally bound to a body. As Descartes puts it, "this 'I', that is to say, the soul by which I am what I am, is entirely distinct from the body."[65] The ancient philosopher Plato went further, seeing the body as the "prison" or "tomb" of the soul.[66] With Plato, we find ourselves in the foyer of Gnosticism, famous for its disdaining the body outright, along with all material reality, as inherently evil.

According to this anthropology, the body with its biological hardwiring weighs upon the soul as an albatross, and stands as an inimical threat to the autonomy of the thinking, choosing "self." Reflecting upon the traction that this anthropological account has gained in modern times, the noted author Wendell Berry observes how this view "look[s] upon the body, as upon the natural world, as an encumbrance of the soul, and so hate[s] the body, as (it) hate[s] the natural world, and long[s] to be free of it."[67] Considered completely malleable, the body must be exploited and conquered, if only to free the soul from its bonds, or recast to fit unbridled, solipsistic free will. Descartes himself expressly asserts that the goal is to "make ourselves as it were the masters and possessors of nature"—and, by extension, the masters and possessors of our embodied nature.[68]

The modern secular approach to sexual choices and lifestyles is largely predicated on this Cartesianist, or *dualist*, anthropology. We know this because of the attitude taken toward our biological hardwiring. Today the biological ordering to procreation is largely seen as impertinent—if not outright hostile—to sexual love (unless we choose to make it otherwise) and as placing no inherent moral obligation upon us. Sex, for the most part, is an affair of internal desire and love, with the biologically structured body standing on the outside looking in (save for the pleasure enjoyed).

In his same year-end address to the Roman Curia that was cited earlier, Benedict XVI notes that today's "new philosophy of sexuality" denies the fact that "bodily identity serves as a defining element of the human being," and instead conceives of the human being as "merely spirit and will." Consider, for instance, how Benedict's assessment resonates in what the first director of the Johns Hopkins Gender Identity Clinic said of transgender individuals at the clinic's opening in 1966: "If the mind cannot be changed to fit the body, then perhaps we should consider changing the body to fit the mind."[69] Or consider Pope Benedict's remark in light of the fact that taking biology seriously (as, say, when we insist that one's sexual self-identity, or gender, must be linked to one's biological sex) is now seen as tantamount to bigotry. Possessing no inherent moral worth because it is non-essential to our human identity, the body can be molded like clay to fit purely utilitarian purposes, or treated recreationally, like a toy or like a morally neutral playground. Consent, nebulously defined and provided by the "self" (the soul), meets the only necessary condition for morally acceptable sexual activity.

We should note in passing the irony of the fact that many proponents of a Cartesian-styled approach to sexual choices and lifestyles are materialists who deny outright the existence of the soul. Let no one claim that the new philosophy of sexuality and the anthropology it espouses are not rife with contradictions!

A Cartesianist disdain for the body is not difficult to find in modern Catholic authors and moralists who dissent from HV and from the Church's teaching on sexual love, marriage, and family. Their disparaging references to "biological function" and "procreative/physicalist processes" give away their bias. One author, for instance, tells us that Catholic moral teaching is driven by an "obsession" with the "mechanics of the procreative process."[70] Another takes issue with the way the Church takes "biological givenness as normative," and a third proposes a moral theory that goes "beyond physicalism."[71] Still another (a gay priest activist) assails the view that discounts certain forms of sexual relationships "that have no possible procreative function," while another accuses the Church of "reduc[ing] sex to a mere biological function" and of "turn[ing] human sexuality into a barnyard-animal affair."[72] Others take a softer position on the body, but make clear their harboring of a Cartesianist anthropology in their disregard for the procreative purpose of sex—even as they do so, spurious as the claim may be, in the name of natural law.[73]

We should not be fooled here. The charges of "physicalism" or of "excessive" importance placed upon biological processes and ends (biological determinism) camouflage an underlying Cartesian bias against the physical or biological order. How else to interpret such language—"obsession with the mechanics of procreation," "barnyard-animal affair"—than as expressive of a "war" on procreation, of a war on biology and the body? Descartes's dream of our becoming "masters and possessors of nature"—in this case, masters and possessors of our bodily sexuality—has been realized. Not mincing words, Benedict XVI quite rightly charges this approach to sexual practice as tantamount to a veritable "debasement of the human body" and a "hatred of [human] bodiliness" (*Deus Caritas Est*, 5).

Integrated Whole or Fragmented Parts?

There stand before us, then, two anthropological alterna-
tives, each defined by its distinct regard for the human body:
either the human body is God's artistic masterpiece, the
temple of the Holy Spirit, or it is a biologically structured
accessory fit for a barn. If the former sees the human being as a paradoxical unity, as an integrated whole, the latter
reduces the human being to a "fragmented self," to use the
term that St. Augustine employs when describing his earlier
life of sexual dissipation in the *Confessions*.

The Church, to repeat, has cast its lot with the view of
man as a paradoxical unity. And with good reason, since
this view coheres both with a proper metaphysics of human
nature and with the revealed biblical view of the human
being. What emerges from this integrated anthropology, as
indicated earlier, is the entirety of Catholic moral teaching,
inclusive of the meaning and purpose of sex.

That said, we must now push this forward. We must now
consider, in other words, how the Church's account of the
moral meaning and purpose of human sexuality, to which
HV testifies, does indeed reflect the truth of human nature.
Let us examine, then, how our sexuality is particularly expressive of our body-soul composite nature, and how this
bears on our moral responsibility to act in view of genuine
human flourishing.

II. The Ordering of Sex to Procreation and Unitive Love

Embodied Complementarity and the Ordering to Procreation

That human sexuality follows primarily upon our embodied
nature is plainly obvious. Because they are linked to the

animal kingdom, our bodies are by their very design of a sexually complementary, dimorphic (male-female) sort, deriving specifically from the genetic karyotypes of XX for females, and XY for males. Without this biological complement, which accounts for all respective physical sexual characteristics (genitalia, bone and muscular structure, breast formation, larynx and beard development, etc.), it is nonsensical even to begin to speak of sexuality. Sex cannot be affirmed, say, of angels or of God, because neither angels nor God (except in reference to the Incarnation) have bodies. We do. And so we are sexed.

Thomas Aquinas observes that certain essential human attributes (he calls them *proper accidents*), although not entering into the formal definition of man, nonetheless follow necessarily upon our rational-animal-like nature. That is, they follow upon the essential constitutive parts of our nature—namely, upon our having an animal-like body and a rational soul. As an example of a proper accident that follows upon our being rational, his points to risibility, and as an example of a proper accident that ensues upon our having animal-like bodies he chooses male-female sexuality.[74] Human sexuality, inclusive of our affective loves and desires, necessarily implies embodied altereity, embodied *complementarity*.

Although this point may seem incontrovertible, especially as we consider it in light of the entire animal kingdom, we should not take it for granted. Indeed, one would search in vain for references to human bodiliness in various Cartesian-styled definitions of human sexuality that circulate today: "Sexuality refers to an intimate aspect of identity through which human beings experience an understanding of self and connectedness to others, the world, and God," is how one of them goes.[75] The point holds as well for those Catholic moralists, otherwise in good standing with the

Church, who locate the ground of human sexuality not in our embodied animality, but in the Trinitarian relations; sexuality, they argue, is first and foremost expressive of a personal relation—namely, the relation of man and woman, as reflective of the relations of Father, Son, and Holy Spirit—rather than as expressive first and foremost of our embodied, animal-like nature.

That human sexuality as an embodied reality is teleologically hardwired for a predetermined particular end, namely, procreation, is plainly obvious. As with most animal species, human generation occurs through the union of two members of the species—two complementary members that together (and only together) possess the power of generation.

Unless we wish to abstract biology outright from our sexed nature, it is impossible to deny or dismiss this. Male-female sexual dimorphism, looked at on the level of strict biology, targets procreation in the same way that respiration targets the oxygenation of blood—to borrow the analogy of one author who points out the absurdity of denying the natural biological purpose of sex when we would never deny this of any of our other natural powers:

> Sex is the only natural power about which we [deride the purpose of nature]. The purpose of respiration is to oxygenate the blood; apart from it there would be no reason to have lungs. . . . If we are consistent, we will reason this way about sex. We will say that its purpose is to generate posterity; apart from this purpose there would be no reason for sexual organs. Instead of saying this, we interrupt the argument to say that the purpose of sex is pleasure. . . . Suppose a young man is more interested in using his lungs to get high by sniffing glue. What would you think of me if I said, "That's interesting—I guess the purpose of

my lungs is to oxygenate my blood, but the purpose of his lungs is to get high?" You'd think me a fool, and rightly so. By sniffing glue, he doesn't change the purpose built into his lungs, he only violates it.[76]

And there we find it stated: pleasure as the primary purpose of sex, as per today's new philosophy of sexuality. Of course, if the Church instead gives priority to the ordering of our sexuality to procreation, it comes not out of some kind of contempt for pleasure, as modern authors are wont to suggest. Indeed, such an accusation is patently absurd, since without pleasure few would find interest in the very act from which procreation follows. Further, pleasure is natural, and God is the author of all things natural. Yes, the Church recognizes the goodness of pleasure, but only as a subordinate good. Nature orders our sexuality to a higher good—procreation—to which pleasure is secondary. Just as the pleasures associated with eating and drinking are a means to the higher end of preserving the life of the individual, so sexual pleasure acts as a means to the higher end of procreation, which ensures the continuation of the human species.

The Body Matters

Here it must be stressed that if the Church harbors an "obsession" with the "mechanics" of procreation or with "biological givenness," to quote again those Cartesian-styled authors we cited above, it is because the Church seeks to honor and respect the human body. Committed to a biblical view of creation and to an Aristotelian view that matter enters into the essential definition of all things, the human being included, the Church refuses to shortchange our biological hardwiring. By giving priority to the procreative (biological) ordering of our sexuality, the Church (with Paul VI serving as mouthpiece) indicates its esteem for the nobility and sacred dignity of the body.

The nobility and sacred dignity of the body derive, of course, from the inherent moral worth it enjoys. Because the body marks a constitutive part of every human person, the Church understands that what we do to our bodies, we do to our very selves as persons; hence the Pauline charge to "glorify God in your body" (1 Cor. 6:20). Put negatively, to abuse our bodies, particularly in its sexed design, is to commit a gravely immoral act, since this is to abuse our very selves as persons. Misusing one's sexual organs, as when engaging in contraceptive sex, is tantamount to, say, misusing one's head to hammer a nail. No one would deny that this latter act is gravely abusive, since, deep down, most people intuitively know that their bodies are integral to their human identity. The body in all of its parts (whether the sexual organs or the head) shares in the moral worth and responsibility of the human person.

So if the Cartesianist, fragmented anthropology that drives the modern secular vision of human sexuality favors, as Benedict XVI suggests, an underlying hatred of the human body, particularly in its biological structuring, then it is no less true to affirm the converse: the integrated, body-soul anthropology, from which the Catholic vision of the meaning and purpose of human sexuality flows as from a wellspring, champions the body. The Church, truly, promotes a love of the human body—God's artistic masterpiece.

Face-to-Face: the Ordering to Unitive Love

By giving priority to sex as an embodied reality, the Church does not intend to signal that sex serves no purpose other than procreation, let alone to undersell this other purpose. As the human being is no mere body, so neither is human sexuality merely expressive of our embodied nature, nor ordered simply to a bodily good. After all, if we say human sexuality is ordered exclusively to procreation, we in no way distinguish human sex from purely animal sex.

That we know there is a difference—a radically profound difference—is betrayed by the distinctive phrase we use to signify sexual union among humans: "making love," a phrase we would never use to signify sex among animals. Indeed, the very physical manner of sexual union among humans, namely, frontal and face-to-face—unique in the animal kingdom—in its own way testifies mightily to this difference. Further, humans engage in sex at will and for an extended duration, also unique among the animal kingdom. What is more, animals always derive the gratification they seek in coitus, but humans often come away from sexual encounters unfulfilled emotionally and with a foreboding sense of moral or spiritual emptiness. Animals do not plod the "walk of shame" after a sexual encounter (an experience not hard to find on college campuses), nor do they attempt to cover themselves when caught with their nakedness exposed (imagine how silly this would look!).

What this indicates, of course, is the fact that in human sexual encounters there is, or at least should be, something much more than the mere physical union of bodies. The sexual joining of two human beings encompasses not simply a physical union, but an encounter of persons, or what John Paul II calls in the theology of the body a *communio personarum*. How else to look upon the bodily frontal posture of face-to-face than as expressive of a union that serves spiritual, moral, and emotional needs in addition to physical needs?

Human sexuality thus enjoys an ordering not merely to procreation but also to a complementary, love-making union. Because this latter ordering is proper to us as rational beings, as persons, moralists term this the *unitive* ordering, though the older classical tradition uses other equivalent terms, such as *domestic fellowship* and *union of souls* (Aquinas), or *conjugal love* and *life partnership* (Augustine).

We can say more about the face-to-face bodily position and how it symbolizes the elevated nature of human sexual union. Recall that "face to face" is the image Paul uses when addressing the ultimate destiny of man, and thus the ultimate meaning we can ascribe to our humanity (see 1 Cor. 13:12); namely, the attaining to beatific glory, or to the immediate beholding of the Triune God "face to face," "for we shall see him as he is" (1 John 3:2). Only in the immediate vision of God "face to face" shall all human desire, bodily and spiritual, find complete and everlasting satisfaction. The sexual union of man and woman "face to face," in its own faint yet privileged way, points toward our final aim, toward supreme human glory.

In short, sexuality as characteristic of the animal kingdom becomes so profoundly integrated in the human condition that it undergoes a thorough transformation. Our bodies in their very physical design bespeak the rational souls to which they are substantially joined, and thereby stand apart from all other animal bodies even as they continue to resemble them (think of Aquinas's view that the human body is designed to fit the rational soul). Just so does our sexed nature participate in and reflect that which is unique to us— our rationality—even as it continues to link us to the animal kingdom (in *Casti Connubii* 7, Pius XI affirms how "reason and free will" shape the unique character of human sex).

Consider, for instance, the ability of the human body, given the unique design of the innominate bone (hipbone), to stand upright and erect indefinitely—a feat no other animal can accomplish. Or how the human hand with its opposable thumb serves more than a mere "animal" need to eat: it serves the proper *human* need to prepare and share in a meal (animals do not experience mealtime). And so it is with the frontal, face-to-face posture of human sex. We are not centaur-like creatures—half rational, half bestial, with a clean line of separation between the sub-rational and rational spheres. We are integrated unified beings comprising both rational and animal dimensions. It bears repeating: the human being is inseparably one.

A Great Paradox

To say human sexuality enjoys an ordering to both procreation and to unitive love is to place us at the crux of *Humanae Vitae*, of the Catholic vision of human sexuality as a whole. As sex is intended to generate human progeny, so at the same time is it intended to unite in love a man and a woman in the most intimate of unions possible. Human sexual union is (or is meant to be) at once physical or bodily and spiritual or moral. To express this in the terms of the metaphysics of human nature, of the fundamental structure of our humanity examined above, the procreative ordering of our sexuality follows immediately upon our embodied, animal-like nature, and the unitive ordering follows immediately upon our rational nature. Georges Cardinal Cottier thus dubs human sex the "great paradox," since it reflects the paradoxical union of body and soul in man.[77] With good reason did Paul VI, given the inseparable connection between body and soul in the human person, insist that there is correspondingly an "inseparable connection *(nexu indissolubili)*, established by God, which man on his own initiative may not break, between the unitive significance and the procreative significance" (HV 12).

The next step is a foregone one. Because sex, as owing to our body-soul composite nature, possesses a two-fold per se ordering to procreation and to unitive love, we can say it has an intrinsic teleological ordering to marriage.[78] Only marriage unites the procreative and unitive dimensions, corresponding to the indivisible, substantial union of body and soul. Human sexuality has a nuptial "grammar" written into it.

Marriage thus marks the normative good of human sexuality. *Marriage*, nuptiality, names the essential meaning and purpose of human sexuality. And what a purpose it is! Because marriage adds the oneness of flesh to the oneness of hearts that typifies all friendship (since to say unitive love is to say friendship), sex elevates union in friendship to an unparalleled, privileged level. Little wonder Aquinas assigns the friendship of husband and wife the rank of *maxima amicitia*, highest friendship.[79]

III. Biblical Confirmation

What we have outlined above argues for a position on the meaning and purpose of human sexuality that is accessible to human reason as such, since it is yielded by the changeless nature of man, by the fundamental structure of our humanity as reason on its own can grasp it. This vision of sex requires no more adherence than to the philosophical view that the human being is a body-soul composite unity. The Catholic intellectual tradition, of which Aquinas is the most celebrated proponent and the *Catechism* is the most recent example, has long held that this philosophical anthropology is best understood in light of the Aristotelian view that all things are composed of matter and form.

At the same time, Catholic moral teaching appeals not only to human reason in propounding its vision of sex and marriage, but also to the authority of the revealed word of God (see again HV 4). Because God is the author both of the changeless order of nature and of the sacred Page (as the medievals called the Bible), we find fundamental harmony between the natural and revealed orders. And, indeed, we need look no further than the opening chapters of the book of Genesis for confirmation of how human sexuality is ordered to the joint goods of procreation and unitive love. At its very outset the Bible offers divine instruction on the nuptial grammar of human sexuality.

"Fill the Earth"

Among the opening verses of Genesis we find these lines signaling the ordering of human sexuality to procreation:

> So God created man in his own image, in the image of God he created him; male and female he created them. And God blessed them, and God said to them, "Be fruitful and multiply, and fill the earth" (Gen. 1:27–28).

With these arresting words, utterly unique among ancient creation accounts, the biblical witness establishes the male-female anthropology (sexual dimorphism) as the norm of our sexuality. Genesis makes clear that we possess the ability to "be fruitful and multiply" only because God, the author of nature, has endowed his human creatures with sexually dimorphic animal-like bodies, that is, only because "male and female he created them." God's creative handiwork establishes complementarity, with procreation as its intended end, as the defining mark of our embodiedness, and thus as the normative good of our sexuality.

We should also stress how the command to "be fruitful and multiply" makes explicit the fact that God "blesses" as good and sacred the procreative design of our sexuality. By naming the sexed design of our nature as among those things that issue from the supreme goodness of God's creative will, the Bible distances itself from a Cartesian-like disdain for the body. Instead, it approximates a view closer to that of Aquinas (the body as God's finest work of art) and Dante (the body as a glorious robe for the soul). Paul's calling the body the temple of the Holy Spirit makes this unambiguous.

"A Helper Fit for Him"

Altering course somewhat, in another remarkable lesson relative to the moral meaning and purpose of our sexuality, the second creation account places the focus squarely upon what we have called the unitive dimension:

> Then the Lord God said, "It is not good that the man should be alone; I will make him a helper fit for him." . . . So the Lord God caused a deep sleep to fall upon the man, and while he slept took one of the ribs and closed up its place with flesh; and the rib which the Lord had taken from the man he made into a woman and brought her to the man. Then the man said, "This at last is bone of my bones and flesh of my flesh; she shall be called Woman, because she was taken out of Man." Therefore a man leaves his father and his mother and cleaves to his wife, and they become one flesh (Gen. 2:18, 21–24).

The biblical witness here presents our sexuality as a gift from God to provide us with a means for attaining oneness in the deepest bonds of human love or friendship. But as this passage's pivotal terms *man* and *woman* unmistakably intimate, the unitive dimension is firmly imbedded in our sexually dimorphic design, in our being "male" and "female" (Gen. 1:27). "Male and female" is God's first response to the human need for friendship, the first response to his fashioning us with a social nature, if only because God intends that in this friendship the oneness of flesh is to complement the oneness of hearts. Recall that when the first man finds no true companion among the animals (Gen. 2:20), God fashions not another man, but a woman.

The Normative Good of Human Sexuality

Taken together, then, the two biblical creation accounts echo what we established above philosophically: namely, that God has endowed his human creatures with a sexed nature for the twofold (yet inseparable) purpose of procreation and unitive love. The Genesis creation account affirms that human sexuality is a gift from God ordered to marriage, which alone joins the procreative and the unitive. Put negatively, the body is meant for no other form of sexual intimacy than that between husband and wife, in an embrace of procreative-unitive love. The book of Genesis thus establishes marriage as the normative good of our sexuality. As John Paul II puts it, the biblical creation narratives lead to "the discovery of the 'spousal' meaning of the body in the mystery of creation."[80]

Although the scope of this essay does not allow for a fuller treatment of the biblical vision of human sexuality, I will simply add that the biblical witness as a whole amplifies the view that God has endowed man and woman with a sexed nature for the express purpose of conjugal love, that is, for a union defined by its joint procreative and unitive purposes. Speaking generally, those acts that violate either or both of the two purposes of sex, procreation and unitive love, are typically condemned in somewhat coarse and crude or immodest language (e.g., "playing the harlot" for fornication [Lev. 21:9], or "uncovering nakedness" for incest [Lev. 18:6]), whereas the procreative-unitive embrace of husband and wife is referred to in modest and circumspect language (e.g., the man "knowing" or "going into" his wife [Gen. 4:17 and Deut. 22:13]), as per a good and sacred act, a holy mystery. In short, what we find propounded in both Old and New Testaments can be termed a morality of conjugal love.

IV. Dehumanizing Sexual Practices

Willing to risk appearing retrograde and out of step, because it refuses to forsake the integrated anthropology from which its moral teaching flows, the Church remains resolute in holding up marriage as the normative good of our sexuality. To affirm, with Paul VI, the "inseparable connection" between the unitive and procreative orderings, is to affirm the inseparable union of body and soul. Here the moral principle of an "ought" deriving from an "is" (the moral equivalent of the scholastic maxim *agere sequitur esse*, "action following being") comes into play. In other words, from the fundamental structure of our humanity, from what human nature "is" constituted by, derives the moral goodness of human action, and thus how the human person "ought" to act.

As man "is" a body-soul composite unity, so his actions "ought" to respect his fundamental structure, at least if he wishes to attain his proper flourishing and happiness. He does this in the sexual arena by honoring the procreative-unitive nature of sex. Further, although we can, and must, distinguish the procreative (as expressive of the body) from the unitive (as expressive of the intellectual soul), we can no more separate these two than separate body from soul.

Yet immoral sexual practices attempt just this separation. Whether in the form of non-procreative acts (artificial contraception, masturbation, homoerotic acts, etc.) or non-unitive acts (adultery, fornication, rape, artificial methods of reproduction, masturbation again, "sexting," voyeurism, etc.), the result is the same: dehumanizing acts that deny our procreative-unitive sexed design, and thus our integrated nature. Such acts attempt to further one ordering at the expense of the other, or to pit one purpose in fundamental contest with the other (typically the unitive at the exclusion of the procreative). These acts deny, at least in practice, the fundamental unity of the human being as a body-soul (procreative-unitive) composite. Sins against the body, they are by that fact sins against human nature and against us as persons.

Those who hold that it is permissible to separate the unitive and procreative purposes of sex do so on an appropriated Cartesianist anthropology. Indeed, this approach that largely undergirds today's new philosophy of sexuality incites us to live not in deferential harmony with our bodies, but to exploit and conquer our bodies, to use or manipulate our sexual organs as a means to enjoying pleasure as the highest good—to be "masters and possessors of nature," to quote again Descartes. It matters not, say, if two bodies of the same sex lack the biological design for true oneness of flesh; all that matters is the mutually consenting "love" between the partners. Likewise, it matters not if heterosexual intercourse is biologically hardwired for conception; all that matters (with the help of technology) is the love the partners share and the pleasure enjoyed, irrespective of this hardwiring. And so on.

Industrial Sex and the Trap of Idolatry

Let us say more about how technology, so central to the contraception debate, has played an unprecedented role in emancipating sexual choices from the constraint of natural ends and of biological hardwiring. So eager is our culture to secure total control of our sexuality that it has rushed headlong to embrace what Russell Hittinger calls "technological hygiene" (Wendell Berry uses the term "industrial sex" to signify the same), by which he means our exploiting technology in order to exert domination over our sexuality.[81] It is no accident, Hittinger points out, that the term our technologically driven culture uses for contraception is birth "control."

At its heart this turn toward "technological hygiene/industrial sex" induces us to look upon technology as a kind of idol, bowing before its awesome power and readily accepting what it deigns to bestow upon us, as if it were *Dominus et Deus*, Lord and God. In this connection, consider the terrifying description of the idolatry committed by the fallen angels before Satan in a memorable passage from Milton's *Paradise Lost* (book II) and how this applies to our own regard for technology:

> Toward him [Satan] they bend
> With awful reverence prone; and as a god
> Extol him equal to the highest in Heav'n.

Toward technology our secular culture bends with awful reverence prone, esteeming it as equal to God, especially in the arena of human sexuality.

Technological Hygiene and the Prophets of Baal

We, in our "awful reverence" for technology, are like the prophets of the false god Baal, who, in their memorable attempt to rebuff the taunts of the prophet Elijah by gaining Baal's attention, lacerated themselves with swords and lances "until the blood gushed upon them" (1 Kings 18:20–40). But as "no one answered and no one was listening" to their "raving on" (1 Kings 18:29), the self-inflicted harm of these prophets of a false god, of an idol, served for naught. It is the same for our own generation's idolatrous eagerness to

avail itself of technological control of the biological structuring of our sexuality, of our determination to force nature
to bend to our will, whether in the form of a techno-pill
(birth control), or of techno-procreation (in vitro fertil-
ization treatment), or of techno-sexual identity (hormonal
treatment for the suppression of puberty and for eventual
"gender change").

The lesson here is that self-inflicted misery and harm are
ever the fruits of idolatry. Looking for in a creature what the
creature does not possess, but which only God does, idolatry
always ends in unresponsive emptiness and nothingness—
and thus in our own demise. Whenever man turns to technology as if it were a god (which, at bottom, amounts to an
idolatrous turn to himself), he finds no one answering and no
one listening. And he ends up covered in his own blood. We
in our "awful reverence" for technology and in our penchant
for playing God have dehumanized and disfigured ourselves
in truly horrifying ways. One need only consider what Paul
VI predicted would follow in the train of widespread contraceptive use to glimpse the bare tip of the iceberg.

Unitive Lovemaking Presupposes Biological Design

The truth of our humanity demands that we treat the body in
all its biological hardwiring as we would any constitutive part
of our human identity. Granted, human sexuality is about
much more than biology, but never does it leave behind our
biological design or somehow make it expendable, any more
than the rational soul leaves behind the material body.

Further, since the body marks a constitutive part of one's
personal identity, the body in its procreative ordering "sets
up" the possibility of unitive lovemaking in the first place.
This exposes as fraudulent the claim that a sexual act that

somehow abstracts from the body's biological hardwiring
can still aspire to unitive love. An act of unitive lovemaking presupposes true oneness of flesh, that is, it presupposes
embodied, male-female complementarity (Gen. 2:18–24
clearly implies as much). Where there is no genuine oneness
of flesh, but instead an inadequate mimicking or a contrived
semblance of it (as with homoerotic practice), there is no full
offering of oneself as a person constituted by a biologically
structured body united with a soul.

Likewise, where surgical sterilization or artificial contraception has sterilized the sexual union of husband and wife,
there is no full offering of oneself as a person constituted by
a (biologically structured) body. In suppressing one's fertility, one suppresses the full offering of one's body or of one's
spouse's body. It is ironic, then, how theologians who dissent on HV often do so putatively in favor of the unitive
purpose of sex, since it is fanciful to speak of contraceptive
sex as genuinely unitive. John Paul II, for his part, was wont
to point out the deceptive nature of contraceptive sex.

We live in a world that ever more resembles that of Shake-
speare's Lady Macbeth, who, Macbeth, you may recall, memorably petitions the "spirits that tend on mortal thoughts" to
"unsex" her in wholly unnatural ways through wholly unnatural acts ("that no compunctious visitings of nature shake
my fell purpose"). How often individuals today, inspired by
secular culture's "new philosophy of sexuality" that rejects
sex as "a given element of nature," seek the same.

Heralding the voice of sanity amidst such madness,
Humanae Vitae offers another vision, another path, another
standard both ancient and new. Embedded within this

encyclical are foundational principles that touch upon the very meaning and purpose of human sexuality, as ensuing upon the truth of what it means to be human. Written into our design as body-soul composite creatures, because it is ordered jointly to procreation (as expressive of our embodied nature) and to unitive love (as expressive of our rational nature), human sexuality is inherently nuptial in meaning.

And so we end with where we began, with the case of Maria Goretti, the "St. Agnes of the twentieth century." Like Pius XII, Paul VI was also concerned about meeting the moral needs of the youth, "who are so exposed to temptation [and who] need incentives to keep the moral law" (HV 17). Today especially, when the determination to be moral in the sexual arena of human life means enduring hostility, ridicule, and possibly even violence, the example of Maria Goretti proves crucial. If HV provides the foundational instruction for keeping the moral law in sexual practice, Maria Goretti—let us call her now the "St. Agnes of the twenty-first century"—offers a concrete model of how to prize the principles enunciated in HV and to live in accordance with them.

We know that the duty to attain moral excellence in sexual practice is incumbent on all, since it flows from our fundamental humanity. Yet, the effort at attaining such excellence will, in today's cultural climate, almost certainly be met with white (if not red) martyrdom. May we find inspiration through the example and the intercession of Maria Goretti as we commit ourselves to this effort.

St. Maria Goretti and St. Agnes, pray for us!

~

3

An Integral Vision of Sex and the Person

Mark S. Latkovic

Responsible parenthood . . . concerns the objective moral order which was established by God, and of which a right conscience is the true interpreter. In a word, the exercise of responsible parenthood requires that husband and wife, keeping a right order of priorities, recognize their own duties toward God, themselves, their families and human society.
—Bl. Pope Paul VI, *Humanae Vitae*, 10

[The pill] is a revolutionary development, probably to be ranked among the half dozen or so major innovations in man's two or more million years of history. In its effects, I believe that the pill ranks in importance with the discovery of fire, the creation and employment of tools, the development of hunting, the invention of agriculture, the development of urbanism, scientific medicine, and the release of and control of nuclear energy"
—Ashley Montagu, *Sex, Man, and Society*[82]

Blessed Paul VI's July 25, 1968 encyclical letter on the
transmission of human life was situated between two event-
ful summers. In 1967, the so-called Summer of Love saw the
sexual revolution explode into view after simmering since
at least the 1950s. The second summer was that of 1969,
when the world watched in awe as three astronauts landed
on the moon. Like the lunar landing, the invention of the
pill in 1960 had indicated the decade's growing technological prowess over the forces of nature. This desire to surmount the limits of man's biology—and indeed his earth-
based existence—had been the goal of modern science for
four centuries, beginning with Francis Bacon.[83]

So it is in some ways fitting that *Humanae Vitae* (HV) was
promulgated in that summer. The long-awaited encyclical
ended up reaffirming the Catholic Church's condemnation
of contraception, causing a theological storm of sorts, including radical and public theological dissent that continues
to this day. On so many levels—ecclesiological, anthropological, theological, and moral, among others—the encyclical was a rock dropped into a river whose ripples have continued for half a century and counting.

A Decade of Revolutions

By 1968, from computers to communications technology to cancer treatment, a scientific revolution was taking
place alongside the sexual revolution that would continue
full steam into the present. Yet this era of "progress" would
come to be seen, on many fronts, as one of decline, deca-
dence, and despair. Just as the scientific and technological
revolution was bearing fruit, the sexual revolution was con-
solidating its rotten gains, becoming part of the mainstream
culture. The so-called counterculture of the 1960s was by
the mid-1970s simply the culture.

But with the rising rates of divorce, out-of-wedlock pregnancy, abortion, illicit drug use, and sexual crime,[84] some were starting to question whether the utopia that the sexual liberationists had promised—wasn't the pill supposed to prevent these problems?—wasn't in fact a dystopia. The discarded women and abandoned children[85] weren't faring so well under the new rules of what became known as the "New Morality." Neither did the scientific revolution, on which secular humanists relied to solve problems like unwanted pregnancies, overpopulation, and sexual inequality with technologies like the pill, fulfill its utopian promise.

Today, with Artificial Intelligence (AI) heralded as the latest techno-savior, the Church never ceases to remind us of both our human and baptismal dignity. Nothing, it tells us, should replace man at the center of human concern and action. In his first encyclical, *Redemptor Hominis* (1979), Pope St. John Paul II spoke of "man's 'kingship'; that is to say his call to share in the kingly function—the *munus regale* of Christ himself" (16).[86]

Let's take in this "call" for a moment: the baptized share in the *very kingly mission of Christ*! Such is the Christian man and woman's great dignity and vocation.

Aware of what he recognized as a time of "great progress," but also of clear threats, John Paul II goes on to lay down a general moral norm to guide the formation of conscience and free choices in the use of technology (and this, of course, would include contraceptive technology): "The essential meaning of this 'kingship' and 'dominion' of man over the visible world, which the Creator himself gave man for his task, consists in the priority of ethics over technology, in the primacy of the person over things, and in the superiority of spirit over matter" (16).

Humanae Vitae and the Personalist Vision

This emphasis on the dignity of the human person would of course be the hallmark of John Paul II's papacy. In fact, his *personalism* would be a key component of what many consider his most original contribution to the Church's moral thinking: the "Theology of the Body." And the latter, in turn, would not only illuminate the reality of the human body as integral to the *being* of the person, but would also complement and further develop the arguments of *Humanae Vitae*.[87] In many ways, the decades after the promulgation of HV would probably have been even more turbulent without John Paul II's defense of the embattled encyclical and related doctrinal matters. We might say that the "integral vision" of man (HV 7) or, if you will, the personalism at the heart of Bl. Paul VI's encyclical, was the "inherent bond uniting sex, love, and procreation."[88] And it was precisely that bond, which Paul VI affirmed so clearly, that John Paul II wanted to explain more fully in his own personalistic theology.

It should be noted that there have in fact been two very different "personalisms" in play since the Second Vatican Council. First, there has been the sort promoted by those who reject HV: a confused view of the person that noted theologian William E. May called a "separatist" or "disintegrative vision" of the person and human sexuality. In this view, for example, there is no bond linking sex with procreation, making contraception is morally legitimate.

Popes Paul VI and John Paul II, on the other hand, in full communion with the consistent doctrine of the Church, proposed a unitive or "integral vision" of man, whose *sexuality reveals his person* and his purpose. In this view, the person is understood holistically and his power to give life is a *personal* reality. John Paul recognized that the anthropology he and his predecessor outlined, contrary to the personalism of the dissenters, present us with "irreconcilable concepts of the human person and human sexuality" (*Familiaris Consortio* 32).

John Paul II's personalism was no radically new kind of philosophical or theological anthropology. Rather, it is rooted in Aristotle and St. Thomas Aquinas, which is to say it is rooted in reality. But it goes beyond these great thinkers to integrate the modern notion of *subjectivity*, of experience and perception, without falling into the modern trap of denying that truth is objective, real, and knowable. He would reject, for example, claims to "your truth" and "my truth" even as these "truths" contradict each other or reality. Now, it is certainly true that we each have a view of the world—a subjective view—that is distinctly ours and is unrepeatable. Even so, any truth that we find in our experience necessarily must correlate with larger truths that lie outside us.

Father Peter Bristow notes that "subjectivity [of the person] refers to everything in the human being that is internal and invisible, whereby each human being is an eye witness of its own self."[89] This does not mean, however, that we grasp the inner workings of our minds by simply peeking into our heads. Rather, "it is by awareness and reflective awareness of the actions" that the person performs.[90] Hence, the title of Karol Wojtyla's most famous philosophical work, *The Acting Person*. John Paul's personalism is the "complement . . . of what Wojtyla calls the cosmological understanding of traditional Aristotelianism and metaphysics."[91]

Where those who reject HV hold up a version of the human person in which one can, in a sense, create his own law based on his own experience, John Paul counters that the human person, through his own experience, encounters God's law as a reality, and owes it to himself and to God to conform his will to this law, so as to live in freedom. At the heart of this personalism is the figure of Jesus Christ, who provides the standard of the perfect man and of morally upright action.

This is why John Paul was so fond of a particular passage from the Vatican II document *Gaudium et Spes* (GS):

> The truth is that only in the mystery of the incarnate Word does the mystery of man take on light. For Adam, the first man, was a figure of him who was to come [cf. Rom 5:14], namely, Christ the Lord. Christ, the final Adam, by the revelation of the mystery of the Father and his love, fully reveals man to man himself and makes his supreme calling clear (22).

Technology and Human Love

Humanae Vitae's view of the relationship between technology and the human person can likewise be understood in the Christian-personalistic framework. Although the encyclical welcomed science that is conformed to sound morality, its view is profoundly different from the technocratic optimism that NASA's achievements came to symbolize for many in the 1960s—the foolish idea that if we can send a man to the moon, we can eradicate poverty, prejudice and every other problem through technological ingenuity and planning alone. For the Church, the only kind of science we should pursue is that which is conformed to both the natural law and the eternal law of God.

Humanae Vitae's understanding of conjugal love, likewise, would be radically different from the "sexual liberation" celebrated in American cities during the Summer of Love. Already, the fathers at Vatican II had warned how this love was a counterfeit when compared to the kind of love that merges "the human with the divine," leading the spouses to make of themselves a "mutual gift" (GS 49) This is why Christian married love "far exceeds mere erotic inclination, which, selfishly pursued, soon enough fades wretchedly away."

What did HV teach about conjugal or spousal love? According to Pope Paul, Christian married love has its origin in God, the author of marriage (HV 8). Specifically, it is a love that is "fully human," involving not only the emotions but also an act of the free will to commit to each other's fulfillment. Spouses become, in a way, one heart and one soul. This kind of love amounts to a total gift of self; it is "faithful and exclusive" of all others; and finally, it is "fecund," in that it seeks to "go beyond" the "loving interchange" of the couple "to bring new life into being" (HV 9). How different from the modern idea that love is a *feeling,* an emotional experience that includes romance, eroticism, pleasure, fun, and so on, and is ordered to self-fulfillment. To such a mindset, children are seen as a burden or, at best, optional accoutrements.

It is again important to emphasize that the vision of love articulated in HV is fully harmonious with the teaching of the Second Vatican Council's *Gaudium et Spes*, as Paul VI explicitly intended it to be (HV 7)—contrary to some theologians who said that the Holy Father was turning his back on the council's teaching by adding fecundity to the council's understanding of conjugal love.[92] As the future Pope John Paul II noted in an important essay just before his elevation to the Chair of Peter, ten years after HV was promulgated:

Even if we note that *Humanae Vitae* rarely uses the term "person," there is nonetheless no doubt that it considers man as person and understands the reciprocal gift of man and woman in marriage in the same way that *Gaudium et Spes* does, i.e., as that reciprocal gift of persons, "who," we read, "mutually give and receive each other" (GS, no. 48). In such a way, indeed, that there arises 'this intimate union, insofar as it is the mutual gift of two persons' (ibid.). By seeking, in conformity with the directives of the encyclical itself (HV, no.7), its bases in an analysis of the concept of love in the Pastoral Council of Vatican Council II, we reach in this way the anthropological vision of the aforesaid Constitution, which is profoundly "personalistic."[93]

The Human Person, Technology, and Moral Virtue

In boldly reaffirming the Church's constant and centuries-old teaching on contraception, HV proclaimed that "each and every marital act must of necessity retain its intrinsic relationship [or remain open] to the procreation of human life" (*per se aptus vitam generandam*, HV 11).[94] Although this personalist moral norm prohibited contraception as an act that is "intrinsically wrong" (HV 14), it did not require of the spouses a procreative *intent* in each and every conjugal act. The Holy See understood that a woman is only fertile during a limited part of her cycle, and it affirmed that marital relations during this window were entirely licit as a means toward preserving and growing marital love.

Further, contra caricatures of Church teaching, HV did not imply that the Catholic Church took a negative view of sexual pleasure—as long as it took place within marriage and in acts that were morally licit.[95] Moreover, as we have already pointed out, HV was not in any way opposed to science and technology: "The Church is the first to praise and commend the application of human intelligence to an activity in which a rational creature such as man is so closely associated with his Creator. (HV 16)" But, "she affirms," the Holy Father continues, that this application "must be done within the limits of the order of reality established by God."

In a word, man must use the gift of technology in such a way as to exercise responsible *stewardship* over creation in all areas of his life, including his own body and sexuality. The moral standard for our use of any technology is whether it serves the true good (and goods) of the human person or enslaves and thus degrades him, and hence is evil. The Second Vatican Council taught, as a kind of first principle of morality: "Hence, the norm of human activity is this: that in accord with the divine plan and will, it harmonize with the genuine good of the human race, and that it allow men as individuals and as members of society to pursue their total vocation and fulfill it" (GS 35)[96] We note here again how this moral norm is entirely harmonious with the personalism of John Paul II, who grounded his anthropology and ethics in Jesus Christ, the second Person of the Holy Trinity, in whom each human person finds his vocation and ultimate fulfillment. Whether one takes the "cosmological" view of ethical norms "from the outside," or a personalist view "from the inside," the ends are the same, guiding each human person based on the law that is written on every human heart to his ultimate goal of flourishing in this life and union with God in eternal life.

As we noted earlier, John Paul II also described this "stewardship" or "dominion" over the created world as consisting "in the priority of ethics over technology, in the primacy of the person over things, and in the superiority of spirit over matter" (*Redemptor Hominis* 16). Only prudence applies the naturally knowable general principles of morality to concrete moral problems. This virtue is closely tied to a well-formed conscience in the Christian tradition.[97]

Grasping the difference between morally acceptable uses of Natural Family Planning (NFP, which limits marital intercourse to infertile periods) and immoral "artificial" birth control methods (i.e., contraception) comes down to discerning

these two contrary ways of understanding technological intervention in the generative process (cf. HV 16)—one of which
works *with* God's plan for generating human life, the other
against it. It also entails understanding the following crucial distinction: couples using contraception and those using NFP to
postpone pregnancy may have the same "further intention," in
not wanting to conceive a child, but their "present intention,"
that is, *what* they freely choose to do in this specific action (or,
in other words, their means to the end) radically differs. In the
language of moral theology, we can say that the "object" of the
act of contraception is always immoral.[98]

In brief, as William E. May and others have argued,
contraceptive intercourse is always *anti*-procreative—ultimately anti-life *and* anti-love. NFP, by contrast, when used
to postpone pregnancy, is merely *non*-procreative—though
its principles can also be employed to help couples achieve
pregnancy when they desire to do so. But where contraception disrupts the mutual gift of self that is at the heart of
conjugal love, NFP preserves and honors it, in turn fostering greater marital communication, harmony, mutual love,
affection, friendship, and fidelity.[99]

A common means of illustrating the difference between
radically different actions that can contain similar desired
ends is in the case of food and nutrition. Let's say two persons
both enjoy a dinner of fine steak and potatoes, and both want
to remain physically fit and avoid becoming unhealthy by
consuming too many calories. Both persons in this scenario
have the same desired ends, or goal, of enjoying good food
and remaining healthy. One person pursues this goal by enjoying a smaller portion while keeping up a healthy lifestyle,
refusing to eat more than is good for him. The other person
has a much larger portion, but purges the meal after eating so
as to avoid the consequences of eating too much.

Both have eaten the meal and have prevented their bodies from having to absorb more calories than they would prefer, but who would think that, because they have both reached their desired ends, that their actions were the same? Would it not be more truthful to note that one acted in conformity with health and the natural ends of eating, while one wanted to eat while avoiding the consequences of the action, resulting in an unhealthy act?

Pope Paul VI articulated in HV the moral difference between these two approaches, teaching that married couples who take advantage of "the natural cycles immanent in the reproductive system rightly use a faculty provided them by nature." When couples engage in contraceptive practices, however, "they obstruct the natural development of the generative process" (16).

"It cannot be denied," the pope continued,

> that in each case the married couple, for acceptable reasons, are both perfectly clear in their intention to avoid children and wish to make sure that none will result. But it is equally true that it is exclusively in the former case that husband and wife are ready to abstain from intercourse during the fertile period as often as for reasonable motives the birth of another child is not desirable. And when the infertile period recurs, they use their married intimacy to express their mutual love and safeguard their fidelity toward one another. In doing this they certainly give proof of a true and authentic love.

Some claim that certain kinds of contraception are not "artificial" because they don't use manufactured hormones or chemicals. Can we not say that a condom made from animal skin, or a contraceptive derived from herbs, are "natural"?

But this misconstrues what makes contraception anti-nature and what makes NFP truly nature-friendly—friendly to human nature and its ends, to the nature of the marital act as God designed it, to a person's (especially a woman's) biological nature, and even to the external natural world.[100] NFP works *with* nature, not against it. It regards fertility as it is regarded in Sacred Scripture: a blessing rather than a curse.[101]

The hermeneutical key to understanding the personalist moral vision of HV, then, is a "balanced" approach to technology, rooted both in its "holistic" anthropology or "integral vision" of man (HV 7, 17)[102] and its call to a virtue-based approach to solving human problems; for example, in its recognition of the essential importance of self-discipline (10, 21) and the virtue of chastity (22).

Thus, the encyclical "urges man not to betray his personal responsibilities by putting all his faith in technical expedients. In this way [the Church] defends the dignity of husband and wife" (18). The pill is one such expedient harmful to man's personal dignity as an embodied soul who is created in God's "image" and "likeness," as either "male" or "female" (cf. Gen. 1:26–27).

At the same time, the pontiff can appeal, without a trace of contradiction, to governments (23), to scientists (24), and to doctors and nurses (27) to develop and employ family planning methods that are sound both morally and medically.[103] Paul VI had great hope for man and his intellect, but he placed his faith in God, who alone provides the grace Christian spouses need to live the demands of a good and holy conjugal life.

The Inseparability Principle

When Pope Paul spoke of the two "meanings" of the marital act—the *unitive* and the *procreative* (HV 12)—he was teaching us, even before John Paul II's Theology of the Body developed the idea, that the human body is an "icon" that not only reveals or expresses the person, but that speaks a special *nuptial* or *spousal* language designed by God.[104] This is the language of *conjugal love*—that is, the language of the "mutual gift of self," of the "union of two persons in which they perfect one another" while also "cooperating with God" in the procreation and education of new lives (HV 8–11, 13). As the theologian Alain Mattheeuws beautifully summarized the point: "To speak of 'meaning' is to indicate, at one and the same time, what the spouses 'want to say to each other' in the conjugal act and that which the act 'says' in itself."[105]

Humanae Vitae's doctrine on the immorality of contraception is based on the insight—derived from "the natural law and illuminated and enriched by divine revelation" (HV 4)—that these "meanings" (or "significances") are "inseparably connected" by God (12). Man is not to intentionally separate them, for to do so is to either violate one or the other value—in truth, really *both* values—for both are "inherent to the marriage act" (12).

In other words, the pope is saying that the marriage act can be described anthropologically as that intimate personal act of the spouses essentially involving, by its very nature as designed by God, a "person-uniting" aspect and a "life-giving" aspect. If you harm one aspect, you harm the other; for both are "interdependent" realities, as John Finnis has argued,[106] reflecting the covenantal nature of marriage.[107] But to act against either or both aspects to violate not only that particular "meaning," but also, Paul VI tells us, the design or plan of God, which is the very norm of marriage (HV 13), as the Magisterium has always taught.[108]

When our contemporary culture's understanding of the human person is erroneously dualistic, separating personal life (the mind, or self) from biological life (the body); when its idea of "responsible parenthood" means to wear a condom in order to have "safe sex," is it any wonder that HV's understanding of sex and of "responsible parenthood" is often ridiculed and scoffed at? That the Catholic Church is viewed as the "bad guy" and Planned Parenthood as the "good guy"? "Why can't we, after all, substitute *techne* for virtue when it comes to sex?" the culture keeps asking over and over again.

It is this last question, more so than the manufactured conflict between the Magisterium's teaching authority and personal conscience, that goes to the heart of a proper understanding of HV.[109] It also reveals, as George Weigel has recently argued, where the Church is most "boldly countercultural," to wit: "in teaching that the morally appropriate means to regulate fertility is through biology rather than technology."[110]

In an unserious culture, however, where comedians and rock stars are looked to as sources of wisdom and utilitarianism is the dominant ethical theory, entertainment and expediency trump virtue and morality. Therefore, like its founder, Jesus Christ, the Catholic Church will continue to be a "sign of contradiction" (HV 18; cf. Luke 2:24). Because the Church, unlike purely secular institutions, looks at human procreation under its natural as well as its supernatural aspects (HV 7).[111] In this way, it does justice to its view of the human person as both created by God and destined for him.

Sanity in a Crazy World

Despite the culture's disregard of traditional morality, many continue to look to the Catholic Church as a credible (and fixed) source of religious and moral truth on account of the truth of HV. It is a remarkable truth, I would argue, at the heart of both the "culture of life" and the New Evangelization. To name but one individual attracted to the Church because of HV, the esteemed British writer Malcolm Muggeridge (1903–1990) spoke movingly about the encyclical already before his conversion to the Catholic faith.[112] It was, he says in his *Confessions of a Twentieth-Century Pilgrim*, the Catholic Church's firm stand against contraception and abortion that finally convinced him to convert.

If Muggeridge were to find himself pope, he wrote ten years after the encyclical's release, his "first venture . . . would be to reissue *Humanae Vitae* . . . reinforcing its essential point that any form of artificial contraception is inimical to the Christian life . . . The divorcement of eroticism from its purpose, which is procreation, and its condition, which is lasting love, consequent upon the practice of artificial contraception, was proving increasingly disastrous to marriage and family."[113]

Paul VI warned of such bitter fruits because the moral norm of the inseparability of the unitive and the procreative ends acts as a safeguard of conjugal love and the natural family, which is the primary unit of a healthy society. Thus HV proposed quite a different way from the prevailing fad of sexual license to create what it called an authentically "human civilization" (18). By "preserving intact the whole moral law of marriage," in showing respect for the physical and spiritual reality of fertility in the context of married love, couples humbly acknowledge that they are "not the master of the sources of life but rather the ministers of the design established by the Creator" (13). Imagine that: spouses are the ministers, the *priests* of God's intelligent love and his creative power to give life—co-creators of new human life with the Lord God himself!

In a world that seems to have gone crazy, HV is a message of personal and moral sanity: the sanity of life over death, of love over lust, and hope over despair. It is, as Pope Benedict XVI said in a May 2008 address to mark its fortieth anniversary, "a gesture of courage."[114] Note too his important words in *Caritas in Veritate* on how HV's teaching is not simply

> a question of purely individual morality: *Humanae Vitae* indicates the *strong links between life ethics and social ethics*, ushering in a new area of magisterial teaching that has gradually been articulated in a series of documents, most recently John Paul II's encyclical *Evangelium Vitae*. The Church forcefully maintains this link between life ethics and social ethics, fully aware that 'a society lacks solid foundations when, on the one hand, it asserts values such as the dignity of the person, justice and peace, but then, on the other hand, radically acts to the contrary by allowing or tolerating a variety of ways in which human life is devalued and violated, especially where it is weak or marginalized'" (15).

With the benefit of five decades' worth of hard experience and social science data indicating the dire meta-level consequences of divorcing sex from procreation, we see ever more clearly that a personal moral norm involving the human person cannot be rejected by so many without serious repercussions. But it all makes perfect sense, really. For contraception, more than preventing "unwanted" children from coming-to-be, *leads us to view children as unwanted.* This selfish attitude is part and parcel of what is meant by the "contraceptive mentality" that John Paul II spoke of.[115] This attitude forms the ethos of the culture of death.

In retrospect, it is clear how compassionate Pope Paul really was to warn the human family about it. If only the world had listened!

Joyfully Personalist, not Dourly Physicalist

As Catholics, we must take the opportunity of HV's fiftieth anniversary to renew our commitment to live its fundamentally joyful—yes *joyful*—message. For it is not fundamentally about a ban on birth control, but rather, a blueprint for a happy life. As Paul VI wrote, echoing the Psalmist, "man cannot attain that true happiness for which he yearns with all the strength of his spirit, unless he keeps the laws which the Most High God has engraved in his very nature. These laws must be lovingly observed" (31). Note well that Paul VI says "lovingly," not *slavishly* observed!

Hence, let there be no doubt, HV's teaching on "the correct regulation of birth" (HV 5, 24) is neither a mere manmade law subject to change nor one merely on the periphery of the Catholic faith. It is rather "a promulgation of the law of God himself" (HV 20). Thus, observance of this law is fundamental to living the Christian moral life in all its fullness. After all, how could an activity that involves the generation of a new human person not be fundamental to the Christian life?

Contra the claims Fr. Charles Curran and other notorious dissenters, Paul VI's references to "biological laws," "laws of nature," and the laws of God engraved in man's nature cannot be reduced to so-called natural law "biologism" or "physicalism."[116] Rather, "the law of God" that animates HV guides the careful and faithful reader toward a God-given *beatitude*.

To this day, however, rejecters of *Humanae Vitae* repeat their argument that its teachings and those of other magisterial documents pertaining to sex and bioethics are overly focused on the *physical integrity* of the act of sexual intercourse, to the detriment of more personal values. They therefore accuse the Magisterium of "physicalism." But of course this charge is untrue. As we have shown, HV is *personalistic* in its approach to contraception: both the unitive and procreative values must be maintained precisely in order to respect the spiritual and physical unity of the human person, who in the marital act offers himself (as a gift) completely to his spouse. There is nothing in HV that supports the claim; yet, in taking this tenuous charge seriously, Pope Paul's successor would add to the Magisterium an incredible depth and breadth of theology once and for all to do away with such arguments.

In *Veritatis Splendor,* an encyclical on the fundamental principles of the Christian moral life, whose twenty-fifth anniversary we celebrate this year, Pope John Paul II took the charge of physicalism so seriously that he devoted a large section to it, in the context of spelling out the nature of the natural law and the human person.[117] In this key section, John Paul argues that the Church does not ignore that man is a rational being whose freedom is self-determining (within certain limits), but it also affirms that the body is integral to the person. Given the weight that dissenters placed on the charge of physicalism, one key paragraph bears quoting in full:

> This moral theory does not correspond to the truth about man and his freedom. It contradicts the *Church's teachings on the unity of the human person,* whose rational soul is *per se et essentialiter* the form of his body.[86] The spiritual and im-mortal soul is the principle of unity of the human being, whereby it exists as a whole—*corpore et anima unus*[87]—as a person. These definitions not only point out that the

body, which has been promised the resurrection, will also share in glory. They also remind us that reason and free will are linked with all the bodily and sense faculties. *The person, including the body, is completely entrusted to himself, and it is in the unity of body and soul that the person is the subject of his own moral acts.* The person, by the light of reason and the support of virtue, discovers in the body the anticipatory signs, the expression and the promise of the gift of self, in conformity with the wise plan of the Creator.

It is in the light of the dignity of the human person—a dignity which must be affirmed for its own sake—that reason grasps the specific moral value of certain goods toward which the person is naturally inclined. And since the human person cannot be reduced to a freedom which is self-designing, but entails a particular spiritual and bodily structure, the primordial moral requirement of loving and respecting the person as an end and never as a mere means also implies, by its very nature, respect for certain fundamental goods, without which one would fall into relativism and arbitrariness (48, emphases added).[118]

Here, in his emphasis on the moral implications of the human person as a union of body and soul, we again see the natural, "external" moral law enter into union with the personal, or "internal" moral law. John Paul clearly understands the natural law not in a physicalist sense, but in a personalist one:[119]

At this point the true meaning of the natural law can be understood: it refers to man's proper and primordial nature, the "nature of the human person" [John Paul II cites GS, 51],[120] which is *the person himself in the unity of soul and body,* in the unity of his spiritual and biological inclinations and of all the other specific characteristics necessary for the pursuit of his end. 'The natural moral law expresses and lays down the purposes, rights and duties which are based upon the bodily and spiritual nature of the human person. Therefore this law cannot be thought of as simply a set of norms on the biological level; rather it must be defined as the rational order whereby man is called by the Creator to direct and regulate his life and actions and in particular to make use of his own body (50).[121]

The extended series of Wednesday papal audiences that became known as the Theology of the Body is a marvelous testament to John Paul II's personalist understanding of the embodied person, and how his body reveals his true nature and purpose. Man in his maleness and woman in her femaleness are created for the "communion of persons." Though we cannot in this chapter consider the full depth and breadth of the theological case made in TOB, we note here briefly how John Paul strengthened the arguments in HV from a personalist theological perspective.

The Language of the Body

The Holy Father in a crucial section draws our attention again to HV's "inseparable connection" (12) language. These words, John Paul II says, "concern the moment in the common life of the couple in which the two, by being united in the conjugal act, become 'one flesh.'"[122] John Paul then states that the human body is "the means of the expression of man as an integral whole, of the person, which reveals itself through the 'language of the body.'"[123] He concentrates on the personalistic aspect of the problem of contraception, and notes that man is "the subject of the natural law in the integral truth of his subjectivity and that revelation shows that he has been called by God to be a witness and inter-preter of the eternal plan of love by becoming the minister of the sacrament that from the 'beginning' has been consti-tuted in the sign of the 'union of the flesh.'"[124]

As ministers of the sacrament of matrimony, "man and woman are called to *express* the mysterious *'language' of their bodies in all the truth that properly belongs to it*."[125] This truth means that the marital act expresses both conjugal love and fecundity. This act is deprived of its proper fullness, however, when its potential fecundity is violated. Therefore, John Paul II argues, "Such a violation of the inner order of conjugal communion, a communion that plunges its roots into the very order of the person, *constitutes the essential evil of the contraceptive act*."[126] It is, to use the memorable phrase that has emerged from John Paul's catechesis on the body, a "lie in the language of the body." Married couples who reject contraception, however, testify to the sanctity of their "conjugal communion."

Those who licitly use periodic abstinence to space births also testify to how blessed they truly are to have integrated NFP into their marriages. It is thus heartening to see that many US dioceses now require that engaged couples take a course in NFP as part of their pre-marital preparation. At Detroit's Sacred Heart Major Seminary, where I teach (as does my esteemed colleague and expert on HV and contraception, Janet E. Smith[127]), all students, including the seminarians, are exposed to the science, morality, and spirituality of NFP in various courses and programs, as well as to the studies indicating its positive effects on marital unity.[128]

I speak from personal experience when I say that this makes perfect sense. When spouses practice NFP, they need to communicate more with each other. This increased communication can lead to not only a deeper bond between them but also to a greater knowledge of and respect for their bodies—their own and their spouse's. This, in turn, can lead to a greater appreciation of their fertility as a personal value. Because of the preceding virtues such as chastity, patience, and temperance, NFP can then lead even to a greater intimacy with each other—physical, emotional, spiritual— and with God.

This is not to say that some couples don't truly struggle with NFP; all do to some extent![129] But not many things in life—especially the good things—come without some level of sacrifice or even suffering. Those challenges can also be opportunities for conversion and human and spiritual growth as individuals, as couples and families. If the moral life were easy, then we wouldn't need Christ, the sacraments he instituted, and the Church he founded!

Those who practice HV's teaching, even amidst great difficulties, are the encyclical's true living witnesses, as well as its beneficiaries. They are helping to build, one marriage and one family at a time, the stable "human civilization" that Bl. Pope Paul VI so longed for us to have fifty summers ago when he gave us the gift of *Humanae Vitae*—a gift that truly keeps on "good-giving," generation after generation.

~

4

Body, Mind, and Soul:
A Couple's Conversion

Jessica and Shaun McAfee

From Shaun

Jessica and I both come from what are, by millennial generation standards, large families. We each had three siblings, though I was the youngest and she the oldest. My father also had three siblings, and my mother, three. Jessica's parents both came from three-child families.

Like most, I suppose, I didn't learn much about contraceptives growing up. Maybe something about the invention of the "purple pill" in US Constitution class. Most of what I knew about birth control came from talks with peers. A girlfriend in high school told me she was on birth control, but we never tested that claim. My parents never talked specifically about artificial contraception, but they did instill in me a strong desire to be chaste and save sexual activity for marriage.

My Evangelical parents also taught with their example. They had four children over the course of five years, with two miscarriages at other points in life. Some time later, I recall a friend telling me of his dad getting "snipped." Now, admittedly, I was not the smartest kid in the world—I was the kid who asked his mother when the fourth of July was and asked his dad how many quarters were in a game of football. I didn't know what getting "snipped" meant, and if I did, it wouldn't have mattered.

My grandparents would shudder to think of sex before marriage, contraception, or abortion. My parents were fallouts of the sexual revolution and the rapid advances in science and so-called "reproductive medicine." The society they grew up in lowered the moral bar little by little. Now, my generation is taught that morality is relative to the choices and feelings of the individual, and the confusion doesn't end there.

From Jessica

Young women are routinely confronted with the decision to take birth control, often long before we are ready even to think about the subject. At fourteen, I found myself facing the decision. I remember how embarrassed I felt when the doctor suggested I go on birth control to regulate my cycle until I "grew out of" the chronic pain, exhaustion, cramps, and nearly constant bleeding that haunted my everyday life. I balked immediately at the idea, "What? No!"

I wanted to know what was causing the pain, not take birth control. I wasn't sexually active. I was committed to sexual purity—what would it say about me if I went on the pill? Who would believe me if someone were to find out and gossip began? Oh, the worries of junior high! Four doctors and one specialist later, I finally agreed to take the lowest-dose pill available rather than fly to a city where I could have exploratory surgery that, even if they found the reason for my physical suffering, wouldn't fix the problem. I wasn't happy about taking the pill, but I was hopeful it would help me to more easily function in regular life.

It made me feel a little better to find out that two of my best friends were also on the pill. They took it because they were told it would clear up their skin. Although this did make me feel like I wasn't weird for having to take a pill for a purpose other than the one it was created for, something always felt "off" about it.

My dad picked up my first prescription. Later he and my mom pulled me aside to go over the instructions. He mentioned that three other parents had been picking up refills for their daughters and were laughing about what a relief it was that their daughters' "acne and menstrual cure-all pill" would also keep them from worrying that their daughters would get pregnant before graduating high school. I was so anxious about what other people might assume about me because I would be on contraception, and my dad's story only increased my anxiety. My parents somehow realized this and told me just how proud they were of me and my commitment to wait for my future husband, and they told me that the fact that I was on the pill would not change how they looked at me, because they trusted me.

The pill did help me with a few of my most worrisome symptoms but it also gave me new symptoms: nausea, extreme food aversions for weeks at a time, extreme lack of energy, and fits of crying (I'm not typically a crier). My body felt like there was an invisible physical burden I carried everywhere with me, like there was a pressure building up in my body that needed to be released. Mentally, I felt like I was living in a fog and basic tasks took far more work, time, and concentration to complete than they should have. I do believe the doctors had my best interests at heart—they worked with my diet, had me record my pain levels, and were sorry they couldn't offer more hope. At least some of my symptoms were gone, so we all counted that as a win.

My first experience with the pill began with a compromise. And though my reasoning was innocent, much like how one small lie tends to snowball into a bigger lie, this was just the first of many compromises that the use of contraception brought into my life.

From Shaun

As an Evangelical Christian, I took my faith very seriously. Nothing mattered more than having a personal relationship with Jesus and committing myself to holiness.

The idea of a personal relationship appeared simple enough, but over time the idea of holiness and sin became problematic. According to my superiors I was "already forgiven," and even if I continued to stumble in sin, I was "always saved." Not only this, but most of the Christians I knew—and that includes the pastors I trusted—disagreed on various points of moral teaching. Some would say that alcohol and dancing were sinful—they'd even tell me it was "in the Bible." Others would say the opposite, also referring to the Bible as their proof.

Was it always wrong to have an abortion? "Of course," some would tell me. Others would tell me there were special cases where there was no other choice. Was it wrong to use birth control? I rarely heard an argument that it was, and worse, I never heard it brought up from the pulpit. Not once.

At the time, I was comforted by the ambiguity. It seemed perilous not to have an abortion in the case of rape, incest, or other hard cases, and it appeared backward to think that birth control was morally wrong.

I was in the US Air Force at this point, in my early twenties, and of course I enjoyed the company of pretty women.

A girlfriend I had at the time, weeks into our relationship, told me she was pregnant. It couldn't have been my child, but she told me she was having an abortion. I told her that I would support whatever she did, but my wish was for her not to go through with the procedure. As things would turn out, she made up the pregnancy so that we would break up, but the question and my unsure response haunted me. The moral weakness I showed was typical of a generation of Christians who don't know why they hold the moral beliefs they do.

In my mind, abortion was wrong. But the sense of culpability, the wrongness, the act of sin and weight of any moral guilt, was mine alone. Others, well . . . they were free to do as they wanted. That is the point of free will, right? If people cannot be free to sin, it seemed to alter the whole Christian worldview of sin and salvation. I didn't feel I had the right to comment on the moral decisions of others, to judge or justify their actions. My morality was mine, theirs was theirs. I owned my own choices, and whatever others did, so long as it didn't affect me, might be disappointing, but didn't affect me. Though I didn't know it, I was a relativist.

From Jessica

As a teenager, there was much to sort out about sex and all of the different points of view to which we were exposed. Even though adults rarely talked to us about it—outside of simply encouraging us to save ourselves for marriage—their worldviews and their families gave clues and ideas on the topic. Whether parents like to think about it or not, even the most sheltered kids will talk with peers about what their parents are teaching them, and are often left extremely confused. Because few of us could approach our parents for help due to the sheer awkwardness of the topic, we were left to our own devices in coming up with our own beliefs.

Some taught that our bodies and the union of our bodies within marriage were created by God as a beautiful gift worthy of protection, and that spouses should respect and desire each other equally. This made sense to me: I was never one to believe that sex is somehow shameful even in marriage. After all, the Song of Solomon is full of delight and the sexual desire of a bridegroom and his bride.

Others believed that sex was only for creating babies and not at all for physical pleasure or unity. In fact, some taught, this type of pleasure was sinful and to be avoided and repented of.

There were also those who believed a woman should never say "no" to her husband, lest she fail at being a good and submissive wife. Furthermore, if she were to refuse his sexual needs at any time she was giving a foothold to the devil to come tempt her husband with pornography, masturbation, lusting after other women, or worse, having an affair. Just imagine what kind of fear and doubt such a belief would cause a woman to live with, even if somewhere down deep she knew it to be false! As if men have no self-control and are mere animals and slaves to every whim, instead of strong leaders capable of putting their wants aside for the good of their families.

The only groups that seemed to be against contraception were certain Catholics and Evangelicals who had ten or more children. I didn't know many Catholics but the stereotype was that they had a lot of children. None of the ones I knew had more than two or three kids, so I had no idea where that stereotype came from. I did know of several Protestants who seemed happy to have so many kids and, in fact, wanted more.

So contraception seemed to be more or less a personal preference, and it was extremely rare to even hear it mentioned by a pastor or other authority. Each of these various schools of thought on sex seemed somehow flawed, incomplete, or unbalanced, but I couldn't put my finger on how, where, or why exactly.

I had no clear teaching available to form my opinion on the matter except that, thankfully, my mother did teach me that some hormonal contraceptive methods could be abortive if they didn't actually prevent contraception. So if I were to go on birth control while married, I should find a method that would truly prevent conception and that could be stopped should a baby be conceived. So when I was married, that's what concerned me the most in choosing a method of contraception. In my mind, *not* being on birth control wasn't even an option.

From Shaun

In 2011 we moved from Fairbanks, Alaska to Omaha, Nebraska for a new job and a new life. A couple months before moving, I told Jessica just before bedtime, "You know, I think I would like you to stop taking birth control. I'm ready to start a family." I couldn't know everything that this meant, but I knew it would make her happy.

Because of her love for me, she had put off for years her desire to have children. Why didn't we begin sooner? In anticipation of our early marriage, which we knew would include switching careers and finishing college, we agreed to postpone pregnancy by having her go on birth control. For me, it was more important to make sure I could support my family than to rush into parenthood without a plan.

She had tried three methods of contraception, searching for one that would work without making her feel terrible. The rush of hormones was very hard for her, but it was all for a good cause, right? For me, the goal was to make the topic "out of sight, out of mind." If we were going to reach my educational goals and maintain the integrity of our future family, birth control was a no-brainer.

Add to this the "couples counseling" we both received from pastors and former pastors, during which we learned how money and children were the greatest causes of stress and contributors to divorce. You didn't have to tell me twice that contraception was a smart idea. I was feeling the cultural pressure to reach a certain status via education and a prominent job, with children coming later. Children, we were told, meant the end of fun, financial progress, and the desired freedom of the "young adult" experience.

With my diploma and a good job offer in hand, though, life seemed to be going right—right enough to start a family.

From Jessica

In my early twenties, I met a handsome young man who became my best friend and soon was the man I held others up to in comparison. I was so happy when we were married! Being responsible young adults, we decided to set our family up for success as best as we could—building up savings, getting Shaun through college, and then into a career. Only after that could we could start growing our family.

We decided to put our heads down and work hard to get to a place where we could provide for children as quickly as possible. We discussed options with pastors to get the best perspective and advice. We talked endlessly about "what ifs" like surprise babies or Shaun being recalled back to the military, and we finally talked to a doctor.

I knew I hated the way contraception made me feel and I was against anything that could potentially abort a baby. The doctor convinced us that these were "no longer real concerns" due to advances in contraceptive medicine, and then congratulated us on our smart choices and goals. We decided to take his word for it.

A needle prick later, I had my first application of "the shot," or Depo-Provera.

Shaun apologized to me as we walked out of the office, because he saw immediately how sick I felt from the artificial hormones that had been injected into my body. He said he wished there was a way for him to take this burden instead of me, and assured me that he would work hard for our marriage and future family. We didn't realize the damage that was about to come through this mentality; we were blind to the chains we had willingly put on ourselves in the name of "responsibility."

We had been told that the first year of marriage would be hard. Well, ours was a cinch. The *second* year was the challenge. We began burning out while trying to reach our goals. We rarely saw each other due to work and Shaun's degree program. We had few friends and no church community, and only occasionally took a break to get a cheap meal or see a matinée. We were still in love, still best friends, but we were tired and we weren't making our spiritual lives the priority they needed to be. I was on my third form of birth control in a year because the shot and then later, "the patch," didn't work well with my body. But we eventually made it: Shaun graduated and we were excited about the next step. Then he received a job offer in Omaha, and we were on our way.

I stopped taking birth control, and began waiting anxiously for a positive pregnancy test. The only thing I had to gauge my fertility was an app that monitored my cycle based on pain I felt monthly. We were both so excited and my health was improving every week, even with all the stress of moving. We decided birth control was a thing of the past and began earnestly looking for a church to call home.

If you had told us that in less than a year Shaun would be following God's lead to the Catholic Church, we would have laughed and said "Not likely!" But that's exactly what was about to happen.

From Shaun

It took only one short month to realize that Omaha was a Catholic city. I still remember how, after ordering a pizza my first night there, I found some nuns praying the rosary on TV. I heard myself say out loud, "I will never be part of that God-forsaken religion."

It's funny what happens when we say "never" to God. Within a few months I had some Catholic friends, and began arguing with one of them against the Church. But it was tough to win the arguments when he could show me that the first-century Christian Church had bishops and priests, oral traditions (long before the Bible was ever published), and a teaching body. It was even more difficult when he showed me how the Bible demonstrates the structure of the Church as it exists today, with one at the head (Matt. 16:18), in communion with the other apostles (Matt. 18:18). From the beginning, the Church clarified its doctrine through its teaching body with the use of councils (Acts 15). My friend showed me how the Church Fathers used the word "Catholic" in letters from the second century, and maybe even before the close of the first century.

Each night, after the latest barrage of claims from my new friend, I would go home, flip open my church history books and look to see if what he said was true. And sure enough, even though my books were written by Evangelical scholars, the names, texts, and testimonies of ancient Christians like Irenaeus, Polycarp, Clement, and Ignatius of Antioch were plainly annotated. Infants were baptized, Christians knew each other as "catholic," and they made the sign of the cross. Without an iota of deviation, they also believed that priests were given the ability to forgive sins, they believed that the bread and wine consumed for communion was the real body and blood of Christ, and they persisted in the belief that the bishop of Rome was the vicar of Christ on earth, the pope. These traditions and articles of faith endured with strong evidence and testimony through every age, and it is still the faith of Catholics today.

There was no possibility of reconciling these issues in favor of my Evangelical intellectual formation. To me, it was as if being Catholic were the only full means of accepting Christ as my Savior, participating fully in his sacraments, and believing fully in his bride, whom he promised to protect (Matt. 16:18), and would never allow to fall into error (John 14:26). Therefore, about a year after I declared I would never be part of the Catholic religion, I realized that I didn't want to be Christian if I couldn't be Catholic.

On April 8, 2012, I received the sacrament of confirmation and entered the one, holy, Catholic, and apostolic Church. My relativistic views on morality and indifference about the choices of others would be shaken to the core.

From Jessica

It was overwhelming for me when Shaun began looking into the Catholic Church. I was newly pregnant, diving into the challenge of starting a small business, and working a side job. I was exhausted. Terrified of miscarrying our baby, I received a recommendation to visit the Pope Paul VI Institute in Omaha. The dignity and care I was treated with in their office was unlike anything I had experienced before, and it wasn't just me: they cared for my husband and our baby as well.

The Catholic faith didn't interest me until I became acquainted with the institute. As my trust in them grew, I began to admire their faith and reverence, especially since at the time they were facing possible changes in the law that could cost them their licenses for their refusal to prescribe or refer for contraception. I didn't understand *why* they were against contraception exactly—my own reasons had to do only with how horrible it made me feel—but I admired their commitment to their faith. Even so, I was cautious.

If someone had asked me at the time what I was "protesting" as a Protestant, I would have laughed and told him to get with the times. I didn't identify as a Protestant. I was a *Christian*. I loved Jesus, I'd happened to fall in love with him while growing up in a Baptist/Evangelical family, and to date, I had few complaints, especially as we had become non-denominational and a lot of the unbiblical teachings and rules I had been taught didn't really apply, depending on which church we attended.

Shaun was totally ready to enter the Catholic Church, but I wasn't. I lived to serve God, and I knew my Bible well enough to defend my faith better than most. So when, in January 2012, Shaun started RCIA, I accompanied him. I supported his search for the truth and wanted to honor him as the spiritual leader of the family. Due to my exhaustion, it was all I could do to stay awake through the late evening classes. Our sponsor and the RCIA leaders were amazing, genuine individuals that I almost instantly respected. The pastor of the parish was welcoming and full of joy. Shaun and I began attending Mass together and, though missing the family feel of other churches, I enjoyed the tradition and ceremony.

When it came time for Shaun to join the Church, I met several times with ladies from RCIA over coffee to talk about what I might have missed, or questions that came up from the discussions. The first time they came into our home, they looked around and saw the peaceful artwork hanging on the walls, Scripture quotes displayed around the house, and a statue of the Holy Family we had purchased during our first Christmas together (which I insisted we keep out all year). One of them remarked that I was easily the most Catholic Protestant they had ever met!

In the end I decided I couldn't, in good conscience, join the Church until I was fully convinced of the reality of the Eucharist. Our pastor told me that he respected the fact that I took it that seriously and that he was going to put it in our file that any time I felt ready, I would be allowed to enter the Church, having fulfilled all the requirements of initiation earlier that year. That happened nine months later, on the first Sunday of Advent.

I never looked back, but I was itching—perhaps mostly because of the tremendous influence of the Pope Paul VI Institute—to learn more about the Church's social and moral teachings, especially about contraception and abortion.

From Shaun

Perhaps I joined the Church with a different mentality than some. I was attracted not only by its art, architecture, and expressions of faith, but by its prominent role in history, and its continuity of teaching, too. And though I was undeniably rapt by the logical basis for the communion of the saints and the sacraments of baptism, the Eucharist, and reconciliation, these were not the sole bases of my decision to join the Catholic Church.

The reason I joined the Catholic Church, above all, was because of what the it *is*. The Catholic Church is not a group of common-minded people. The word *catholic* is not just the namesake of the earliest gathering of believers. This Catholic Church is the Body of Christ, without metaphor. As the

Body of Christ, the Church contains the authority to teach, the completeness of the Christian faith, and the presence of a visible structure that communicates its teachings, and transmits the authority of Christ to the apostles and to every age.

When I joined the Catholic Church, I joined with that discipline in mind. It required my *obedience*, even if I did not understand. It required my full membership, even when I don't immediately agree. It required my devotion, even when I don't feel devoted.

So, when I read in the *Catechism* that any act of contraception is "intrinsically evil," I submitted, even if I didn't yet fully understand the teaching (2370). When I read or heard that Catholic marriages are required to remain open to life, I obeyed. And when the Church says that we must take these truths and evangelize the world, I try to, even when I don't feel like doing so.

Because of what the Church is, I can remain faithful, find out the answers later, and conform my intellect and will to the wisdom of a Church that respects my freedom and calls me to form my conscience in accordance with the truth. I can learn to agree, and remain obedient. I have this belief because I have this discipline; I do not merely believe that I am obedient to men, but I am obedient to Christ. He told the apostles, "Peace be with you. As the Father has sent me, even so I send you" (John 20: 21). He did not say, "*Like* the Father has sent me" or, "*Similar to the way* the Father has sent me." That authority that Jesus bestowed on his apostles, I trust.

In my conversion I became completely convinced that the Church, through Christ, was the only infallible communicator of moral and divine truths, and whatever it taught, I wanted to submit to. Not only as a matter of justice, but also because I saw that those truths had to be the path to freedom and fulfillment, since we are made for truth. But I needed to know more about what those teachings were and the reasons behind them. This would play a key role in my responsibilities as a husband and father.

From Jessica

Ten months after the birth of our first child, I joined the Church and was already practicing and really loving Natural Family Planning (NFP). One year into using the Creighton Model Method, I was approached about the possibility of training to become an instructor for the Pope Paul VI Institute, and I enthusiastically agreed—I would do anything I could to bring the truths and benefits of NFP to anyone who would listen.

The training was far more intensive than anything I had previously experienced. Of everything I learned, I was struck most by the fact that the ethics behind NFP flow naturally and logically from the way God designed our bodies as men and women, and our orientation toward love and communion. *Why do we practice NFP? Why is some artificial reproductive technology, like IVF, morally corrupt? Why, when, and how can we as Catholics do things differently?*

Then we dove into *Humane Vitae* and the veil was lifted. I instantly became a student of Pope Paul VI, and was appalled that everything I learned during those sessions wasn't common knowledge. I realized even though I was open to life and I loved NFP, my worldview was still tainted by the effects of accepting the world's contraceptive mentality.

I learned that there is nothing wrong with spacing pregnancies or even preventing pregnancies—through means that don't harm the integrity of the marital act—for good and serious reasons. The Church encourages discernment to make sure that we aren't being selfish in our reasons to postpone or achieve pregnancy: this is *Humanae Vitae's* real and true version of "responsible parenthood" (10).

I also learned another side to responsible parenthood: remaining open to life and respectful of the fact that there is no known method, contraceptive or natural, that is 100 percent accurate in preventing pregnancy, outside of total abstinence. We need to accept that every marital act could result in a baby and know that we would welcome and love that baby, whatever the circumstances.

I learned in more depth the effects of hormonal contraceptive methods, some of which can be abortifacient by preventing implantation of a newly conceived embryo in the uterus. My mom had been right about this! We learned about the corrupt ends of artificial reproductive technology and the immoral practices that surround it. It shouldn't surprise us that after decades of manipulating women's health to prevent the conception of a baby, we now have a market for the manipulation of her body to become pregnant through extremely expensive, immoral, and unhealthy methods.

I was captivated as I learned how Pope Paul VI foretold many of the logical consequences for society if contraception were to be widely accepted, and why it could not be accepted within the Church—and he was right. Individuals and families have been ripped apart by the lie of "sex without consequences." Broken families are now more common than intact ones, and contraception has contributed to countless lives lost through early miscarriage and abortion. Abuse is rampant, even when disguised as pleasure. Many of the same women in the #metoo movement demanding an end to sexual abuse and disrespect of women have made books like *50 Shades of Grey*, a series about a controlling and abusive sexual relationship, a smashing success.

If I learned anything during my time of training and personal reflection with the Paul VI Institute, it's that it is infinitely more freeing to give oneself totally to another in love and trust than it is to rely on a drug to disable our fertility so that we need not suffer the natural and healthy consequences of our free choices. In a loving marriage, we give ourselves to one who isn't going to take off or demand an abortion should a pregnancy occur; someone who will long to look into his baby's eyes and see them as the miracle they are.

I realized that, even while I was practicing NFP, after our first child, I was doing so with the wrong mentality. I had been afraid of my fertility, and that had been holding me back from giving myself as freely and with the openness to life that my husband and our marriage deserved. Since I abandoned the contraceptive mentality of fear, I have never been tempted to return to it. Whatever the cost, living in the freedom of openness is absolutely worth it.

From Shaun

The idea of being a Catholic was initially romantic to me, and it continued to stir my imagination even as we moved beyond that wonderful first Easter season. It did not take me long, though, to see another side of the Catholic Church. I began to tell my conversion story to my Protestant friends and write about the Faith in Catholic circles online. The more time I spent searching for different perspectives, the more the ideal faith I had imagined began to recede. Though I found some who were clearly trying to present the teachings of the Church in a positive way and increase the faith of others, I also found dissent: diatribes against popes and bishops and criticisms of some of the more unpopular social and moral teachings of the Church, especially contraception.

After a few months, a deacon friend who had been integral to our formation in RCIA found me in adoration on a weekday afternoon. I didn't want to waste the opportunity to speak with him, so I caught up with him in the narthex and asked him what he thought about contraception.

"If you're asking what the Church teaches: it's a grave sin. As Catholics we believe that contraception is against the natural law, because it interrupts the purpose of the marital act, which is procreation."

I replied that I was generally familiar with the prohibition against it, but didn't understand why so many Catholics felt free to disagree with the Church publicly, and even attack it for not changing this teaching. I told him that I'd found a fair number of Catholics online defending the use of contraception, and even Catholic politicians supporting abortion. "How can they do that?" I asked him.

"Shaun, welcome to the Catholic Church," he said with a sigh.

I cracked a smile and assured him that, though Jessica and I were already not using birth control, we wanted to actually know and understand the Church's teaching. Deacon Michael suggested that I start with an encyclical from Pope Paul VI called *Humanae Vitae*.

And so I did. *Humanae Vitae* confirmed several aspects of the Church's teaching on sex and responsible parenthood, but it also challenged my assumptions. This was one of the first encyclicals I read as a Catholic and I was impressed by the combination of charity and boldness to preach against grave evils. *This was the Church I joined!* As for the volatility of the debate that followed the encyclical's release, and the near total absence of obedience to this teaching, I was stunned. Nonetheless, this was the Church I joined.

From Jessica

NFP, without a doubt, made me feel better. It allowed me to take control of my fertility, freed me of the side effects of hormonal contraception. This personal experience, combined with the truths that the Church teaches, came in and freed me from a contraceptive mentality I didn't even know I had. Indeed, it set me on a path of freedom in my marriage I didn't know I was missing. It improved my trust and relationship with God to understand a little better how he made me and that my fertility was good—not simply an inconvenient or broken part of being a modern woman.

I had laughed when we talked about marriage-building within NFP because Shaun and I already had a great marriage. I didn't think it needed any more building. I had no idea that it was going to be a continuing process not only of growth and freedom, but also character training and sacrifice for both of us. NFP, no matter which method you choose, is rarely simple or "easy" in practice.

Anyone who has been in an NFP class has heard the sales pitch of the monthly "honeymoon" phase following abstinence during fertile phases. Many couples practicing NFP will raise their eyebrows and say there is usually a feeling of "finally!" But during this same phase, women's hormones also plummet, taking their energy with them. It's a short-lived honeymoon at best. In my experience, I have come to believe that if we teach this "benefit" to encourage use of NFP, we are setting people up for failure by not being honest about the associated difficulties.

When it comes down to it, NFP is a sacrificial system. It's not easy; in fact, it will be an outright struggle at times. The biggest complaint women have is that when we are fertile, it is also the time that we desire our husbands the most. The rest of the month, many women have to work themselves up mentally and emotionally before we can even think about sex. That doesn't mean it isn't enjoyable, only that it can take a little work to get into the right mindset for it and the mood can be fragile. But when we are fertile, we are ready, waiting, and excited for it. This is the one week that, if we are seeking to postpone pregnancy, we find ourselves facing frustration because NFP requires abstinence.

Men, on the other hand, are always fertile, so it makes sense that they are always on alert. Is it more difficult for one spouse than the other? This is hard to say, because always being at that level of readiness has its own set of challenges and temptations. But can it seem unfair, especially to the wives and to the husbands who enjoy the excitement that comes when she is fertile? Totally.

Also, women's bodies are very different from one another's and at different times and ages. What about NFP during the postpartum period, or for women who have constant fertile signs? Certain methods are better than others in these situations and can typically be managed with the aid of a practitioner. But it requires some investment to understand and determine what the woman's body is doing, and that involves some sacrifice and creative ways to make sure we aren't neglecting our spouse's need for intimacy simply because sex is off the table until further notice.

NFP in marriage can create issues: frustration, feeling rejected when one is "in the mood" and the other isn't, feeling pressured, irregular fertility signs and difficulty in charting, to name just a few. Sadly, the most frequent reason given by couples who stop using NFP is the difficulty of even limited abstinence for the men, who often pressure their wives into quitting. These are men who should be growing in self-control and virtue, to whom families should look for leadership and self-sacrifice, and they are robbing themselves and their families of this example. As a practitioner, one solution I offer to couples is that women must have confidence that they won't be pressured, be treated as "the bad guy" or the sex broker, for saying they are or aren't fertile.

This points to the extreme importance of open, loving communication between spouses, and the need for the "always fertile" husband to remain chaste. Neither spouse should have to deal with a cold shoulder when one is ready, but the other is not. Men also need to trust that their wives are charting correctly (or better, cooperate with charting) and not accuse them of using the method as an excuse if they aren't in the mood, or for going against the goals they've mutually agreed to. They also need to gently encourage the basic purpose of the system: responsible parenthood.

If they are to truly aid a couple in their marriage, responsible parenthood and NFP must on a regular basis compel a couple to open up about things they should know about each other and their intentions. At first this may be awkward, but it soon becomes second nature, and the seed that is planted there has the potential to grow into something wonderful. Instead of seeing NFP as unfair to your sex specifically, you can begin to appreciate the sacrifice required of both spouses, each in his or her own unique way.

From Shaun

Yes, I was convinced that the Catholic Church was the infallible communicator of moral truths, but I also needed to unlearn much of what I had thought, and in order to do that, I needed to revise the way I looked at the world.

As I mentioned earlier, I was always against abortion. The trouble was, I had been terribly confused on the application of moral truths. I believed for a long time that the individual alone was the final arbiter of right and wrong. Back then, it seemed to me that if a woman truly believed abortion was right, then it was, *for her.*

The argument is simple to dismantle. All I had to ask myself was, "Why is such a grave moral evil as abortion wrong
for me, but right for someone else?" But in practice it wasn't
easy. Relativism is a powerful, seductive, and deceptive heresy. So many sins of the world hide behind this devious philosophy. As an Evangelical, I had been free to believe that
if I remained immersed in Scripture and prayer, the Holy
Spirit would provide me moral clarity. But what happened
if others arrived at a different conclusion? The Holy Spirit
can't be the spirit of contradiction and confusion. Two passages from the Gospel of John stood out to me at this time:

> *John 14:26*: "But the Counselor, the Holy Spirit, whom the
> Father will send in my name, he will teach you all things, and
> bring to your remembrance all that I have said to you."

> *John 16:7–15*: "Nevertheless I tell you the truth: it is to
> your advantage that I go away, for if I do not go away, the
> Counselor will not come to you; but if I go, I will send
> him to you. And when he comes, he will convince the
> world of sin and of righteousness and of judgment. . . .
> When the Spirit of truth comes, he will guide you into
> all the truth; for he will not speak on his own authority,
> but whatever he hears he will speak, and he will declare
> to you the things that are to come. He will glorify me, for
> he will take what is mine and declare it to you. All that
> the Father has is mine; therefore I said that he will take
> what is mine and declare it to you."

These two passages are utterly clear on the reality of the
unity of doctrine and moral teaching that is provided to the
Church via the Third Person of the Trinity, the Holy Spirit.
As the Church teaches in *Dei Verbum*:

It is clear, therefore, that Sacred Tradition, Sacred Scripture and the teaching authority of the Church, in accord with God's most wise design, are so linked and joined together that one cannot stand without the others, and that all together and each in its own way under the action of the one Holy Spirit contribute effectively to the salvation of souls (11).

No longer was I able to look away from the sins of the world. If an act whose object is intrinsically wrong was wrong for anyone, it was wrong for *everyone*. Any philosophy outside of this is madness, corrupted, but the world continues to be blinded by the attractiveness of relativism. Even in my own short lifetime, we have seen our culture reject the most obvious truths for error, and we have observed the most scandalous of moral acts not only determined to be legal, but even called "good."

Early on in my study of the Church's social and moral teaching, I discovered this profound quote from Cardinal Joseph Ratzinger, who would later become Pope Benedict XVI:

> Today, having a clear faith based on the Creed of the Church is often labeled as fundamentalism. Whereas relativism, that is, letting oneself be "tossed here and there, carried about by every wind of doctrine," seems the only attitude that can cope with modern times. We are building a dictatorship of relativism that does not recognize anything as definitive and whose ultimate goal consists solely of one's own ego and desires.[130]

Because I already recognized abortion was evil, the Catholic Church's clarity in teaching helped me get out of my own relativism, which was a great relief and a help to my reconciliation with God. Next, I had to understand artificial birth control and the corruption of the contraceptive mentality.

From Jessica

When a husband and wife have a loving marriage that is free, total, faithful, and fruitful, it can't help but affect everyone around them. In addition to the grace opened up in the couple's marriage, any children they are blessed with will benefit, as will their own children's vocations and families. When we treat each other with the dignity and respect that being created in the image and likeness of God should entail, we will see our families flourish. Friends and family, and sometimes even strangers, will take notice of our happiness and unity. Sharing how a couple avail themselves of God's blessings is part of the evangelization in which we are all called to participate.

Our character grows through putting God first and each other before ourselves, working as a team, practicing periodic abstinence, and loving our spouse in creative and generous ways. One of the benefits of being an NFP practitioner is hearing how spouses I work with learn to appreciate each other in ways they never have before. By practicing self-discipline and abstinence regularly for short periods of time, we have the opportunity to encourage chastity within our marriage. Self-discipline brings with it the gift for each spouse to flourish in their marriage. It brings peace to the entire household as the husband and wife naturally grow in consideration and thoughtfulness to each other's needs. Children benefit as well, as we parents more seriously carry out our role as spiritual, moral, and intellectual educators.[131]

Now, as true as this all is, I hasten to repeat here that the picture of a loving and peaceful family is hard-won. It is in no way easy or a given—even couples who practice NFP suffer moral failings and misfortune. That beautiful family photo is one moment among many others, most of which are pretty messy and hard. Yet this fact should not dissuade us from the sacrificial love that does, over time, strengthen spouses and a family even in the hardest times. The messy reality of building a faithful family should not lead anyone into an attitude of cynicism.

The character growth evident in couples who practice the Church's teaching on life and family helps to safeguard the family. Were the wisdom of *Humanae Vitae* more widely known and practiced, the epidemic of broken families we see today would be reversed, and divorce would be rare. A shared and sane view of the human person, and the morality fitting the person made in God's image, would be uplifted and encouraged instead of a distant memory, and society as a whole would benefit.

There are other benefits, besides moral and spiritual ones, that have been realized from fidelity to *Humanae Vitae*—especially the great advances in women's medical care and fertility treatments that harmonize with the Church's teachings on life and family. Even single women who have access to NFP can begin charting for their own health, and can seek treatment for the underlying cause of reproductive health problems, rather than missing symptoms being hidden by prescribed birth control. Access to this level of care is now possible thanks largely to the paradigm offered by the Church and to faithful medical professionals who, following it faithfully, have sought solutions in life-giving and life-protecting ways. Like the virtues that flow from a couple's fidelity to Church teaching in marriage, such fidelity on a larger scale has borne much good fruit for the whole world.

From Shaun

After my conversation with Deacon Michael, I read *Humanae Vitae* and learned of the Catholic Church's use of the word "responsible." In the opening lines, the encyclical informs us that, "married persons are the free and responsible collaborators of God the Creator." The document later reads:

> In relation to the biological processes, responsible parenthood means the knowledge and respect of their functions; human intellect discovers in the power of giving life biological laws which are part of the human person.

> In relation to the tendencies of instinct or passion, responsible parenthood means that necessary dominion which reason and will must exercise over them.

> In relation to physical, economic, psychological and social conditions, responsible parenthood is exercised, either by the deliberate and generous decision to raise a numerous family, or by the decision, made for grave motives and with due respect for the moral law, to avoid for the time being, or even for an indeterminate period, a new birth (10).

I was confused as I read this. Our first baby was not even born yet, but this document was telling me that my married life already contained in it the responsibility of parenthood. I had no children of my own! *Parent whom?*

My confusion rested in my faulty understanding of the responsibilities I had to God and to my spouse in the sacrament of matrimony. *Humanae Vitae* clarified this for me:

Responsible parenthood also and above all implies a more profound relationship to the objective moral order established by God, of which a right conscience is the faithful interpreter. The responsible exercise of parenthood implies, therefore, that husband and wife recognize fully their own duties toward God, toward themselves, toward the family and toward society, in a correct hierarchy of values (10).

What this means is that intentionally thwarting the procreative end of our sexuality is wrong because it's a deliberate violation of God's design for humanity. Any and all pleasures that sexual intercourse provides are added blessings from God, strengthening the bond of intimacy, respect, and love between husband and wife while also affording the possibility of creating a new life. Hence we see clearly what the Church understands as the inseparable unity of the dual ends of the marital act. It is not either/or, but always both/and. Even when procreation is unlikely or impossible in a particular act, the essence of the sexual act remains intact when both spouses are truly open to life and do nothing to thwart the procreative aspect.

When we look at the big picture of marriage and sex, the loving environment that is created is the perfect setting for nurturing and educating children. But if sexual pleasure within marriage becomes unnatural, or at odds with how God intended it, it is harmful to spouses.

Unbeknownst to me, when I entered the bond of marriage, I entered into a union with my spouse that was more than a blissful friendship of love and devotion—it was a *sacrament*. And the love we shared was not for us alone—it was made for us to participate in the creation of human life with the Author of life himself! And all the passion my wife and I shared required our mutual self-control, which allows us to offer ourselves as a gift for one another.

We realized how selfish we had been. It wasn't just the use of contraception, but other acts, contraceptive in nature, that had crept into our marital intimacy. We couldn't continue to rationalize the enjoyment of our bodies at the expense of our duty as responsible parents.

These painful realizations informed a deeper examination of conscience, and we approached our priest, confessed, and received absolution. Since then, we've put every effort into ensuring our married life does not conflict with our obligation to be responsible parents, and our assent to the Magisterium of the Catholic Church.

From Us

What's a Catholic to do?

First, we urge you to carefully read *Humanae Vitae* and the many teachings and articles on the Church's social and moral doctrine that help non-experts understand this fundamental teaching. This will help you to examine your conscience and rid yourself of beliefs and acts that are disordered. "Flee from sexual immorality" (1 Cor. 6:18).

For those who have children, pay special attention to Jessica's words. The single most important contribution you can make in the Lord's vineyard is to have and raise faithful, happy, wise, and chaste children. They are the primary benefactors of your responsible parenthood. *Gravissimum Educationis*, Vatican II's Declaration on Christian Education, reads:

Therefore, children and young people must be helped, with the aid of the latest advances in psychology and the arts and science of teaching, to develop harmoniously their physical, moral and intellectual endowments so that they may gradually acquire a mature sense of responsibility in striving endlessly to form their own lives properly and in pursuing true freedom as they surmount the vicissitudes of life with courage and constancy. Let them be given also, as they advance in years, a positive and prudent sexual education (1).

Parents have the primary and inalienable right and duty, that document continues, to educate their children. To educate your children with integrity, you must first be the example. All parents know that you can tell kids not to do something several times, but the one time *you* do it, any teaching you tried to impart can be lost. Second, pray with them—early and often. Their knowledge of and relationship with God begins with how they see you pray. Third, openly and frequently talk to them about moral responsibility in creative ways, stories, and examples. The point is not to drown them in repetition, but make sure they know what it means to make a good decision, and why. If you do these things, you will accomplish the most important task in the vineyard: transmitting the Faith to the next generation.

Finally, for all—for parents, single men and women, professionals, priests, religious, teens, and elderly—educate yourself and continue to deepen your understanding of faith and morals in union with the Church. As his holiness, Bl. Pope Paul VI, urges us in *Humanae Vitae*:

You know, too, that it is of the utmost importance, for peace of consciences and for the unity of the Christian people, that in the field of morals as well as in that of dogma, all should attend to the Magisterium of the Church,

and all should speak the same language. Hence, with all
our heart we renew to you the heartfelt plea of the great
apostle Paul: "I appeal to you, brethren, by the name of
Our Lord Jesus Christ, that all of you agree and that there
be no dissensions among you, but that you be united in
the same mind and the same judgment" (28).

~

5

A Prophetic Witness to Creation

Allan C. Carlson

The appearance of *Humanae Vitae* in 1968 was the most important religious and cultural event of the twentieth century. As a new and yet very old moral darkness was descending on the world, this document altered the course of history. It created the conditions that enabled Christian defenders of preborn and infant life, and of the procreative natural family, to organize and confront the common foe. The conflict continues to our day; indeed, given the deluge of destructive innovations regarding life and family that have been embraced at the heights of culture, things seem to be darker than ever. Without this encyclical, though, the matter would have been decided a half-century ago; the darkness would be complete.

Humanae Vitae (HV) was also a stirring and timely testimony to the natural law. In the face of an ancient but reanimated enemy, it reframed vital truths for new generations. Man is not a soul imprisoned in a body, it affirmed. Rather, he is an inseparable union of body and soul, an integrated being who can rely on his senses and emotions to understand the nature of things and fit into the created order.

True Lessons from the Past

As debate over contraception swirled in Catholic circles in the early 1960s, a central question became: how and when did the Christian opposition to contraception emerge? Legal scholar John T. Noonan's volume *Contraception: A History of Its Treatment by the Catholic Theologians and Canonists*, addressed the question as he laid out an argument for the advocates of change. Although Noonan could not deny that Christian doctrine always condemned, without exception, any attempt to intentionally thwart the procreative end of sexuality, he argued that this doctrine did not grow naturally out of the Gospels and epistles. Rather, he said, it derived from pagan Stoic doctrines and reactions to early heresies, which had distorted or cramped their content: "[T]he emphases, sweep, and place of the doctrine issued from these mortal combats." It was time, he implied, to free Catholics from the resulting sexual "prison."

There is a more accurate reading of the origin of Christian sexual ethics, however; one fully in harmony with HV. This story begins even before Christianity impacted the early pagan Roman Empire, which was marked by sexual and marital disorders. The family-centered virtues of the old Roman Republic were long gone. As historian Robin Lane Fox writes, "*accepted* sexual practice in the . . . empire had a range and a variety which it has never attained since."[132]

For example, the practice of "Greek Love"—sexual relations between a man and an adolescent boy—received literary praise. The early Christian Tatian, who resided in Rome for several decades, reported that the Romans "consider pederasty to be particularly privileged and try to round up herds of boys like herds of grazing mares."[133] Adult homosexuality was idealized as well, often associated with the theater. In the major imperial cities, male prostitution was common

and deemed acceptable. Evidence exists of transvestite practices in Rome, as well, often with a religious veneer, such as
the cult of Elagabalus. Female prostitution was widespread
and socially approved.[134] At the high end of the trade were
dancers and musicians; at the low end, "two penny" women
who worked the street corners and graveyards.

The Roman marriage system was a shambles. When pagan
marriages did occur, the females involved were commonly
quite young. About twenty percent involved child brides of
ages eleven or twelve. Up to half of females who married did
so by age fourteen; the men were, on average, nearly twice as
old. Custom dictated, nonetheless, a quick consummation of
the marriage, even with these pre-pubescent girls.

Roman marital relations were badly strained. Adultery
was widespread and socially acceptable for men. The age
gap between husbands and wives, the access by the men to
prostitutes and slave women, the confinement of Roman
wives in their dwellings, and a male culture that celebrated
cruelty and violence and held marriage in low esteem: as we
can imagine, these patterns rarely produced happy homes.
Not surprisingly, divorce became common, sought by men
and women alike.

Preborn and infant life faced enormous risks. If determined
by the *pater familias*, abortion was legal and common. Illicit
abortions by wives seeking to cover up adultery were also frequent. The fetus had no legal standing. While the poet Ovid
and several other pagan voices raised objections to abortion,
their concern focused on the rights of fathers and the needs
of the empire; they were indifferent to the unborn child. (A
prominent exception was the Stoic moralist, Musonius Ru-
fus.) Abortion kits contained the usual blades, hooks, needles,
and spikes; diluted poisons were also used. These procedures
left many Roman women dead or permanently sterile.

Infanticide appears to have been common. Legal under *pater potestas* (paternal power), male babies with imperfect form and girls were its usual victims. The destruction of baby girls was so common that for every 100 females in A.D. 100 Rome, there were 131 men; out in the provinces, 140. One historian reports that even in a relatively large Roman family, "more than one daughter was practically never raised."[135]

Finally, efforts at contraception were widespread, if often ineffective. Herbs, ointments, and "medicines" were employed, alongside charms and primitive condoms formed out of animal parts.

In short, imperial Rome featured normalized sexual disorders, marital malfunction, and a deep hostility to new human life. Not surprisingly, these characteristics led to a low level of fertility, well below the generational replacement level. Both Julius Caesar (in 59 B.C.) and Caesar Augustus (in 19 and 9 B.C.) proclaimed laws that would punish the childless and reward fathers with three or more children. The measures did not work. "Childlessness prevailed," the historian Tacitus lamented.[136]

It was into this setting of moral darkness and deep hostility toward procreation that the followers of Jesus of Nazareth stepped. Their number was small: still well under 50,000 by A.D. 120. Early Roman observers commonly saw these Christians as simply another burial society, a sort of community fund for burying the dead, with its own ritual meal.

Nonetheless, it soon grew apparent that this Palestinian sect held to startling ideas on sexuality, marriage, and family life. These derived, in part, from a broad acceptance of the pronatalism of the Hebrew scriptures, including their denunciation of onanism (male withdrawal during intercourse). The direct teachings of Jesus on the sanctity of marriage, the sinfulness of divorce, the value of women, the importance and meaning of children, and the broad affirmation of life strengthened this attention to procreative marriage. The letters of the apostle Paul and other early apostolic epistles expanded this new Christian sexual and marital ethic.

Its earliest summary appears in the *Didache*, a manual on church life and discipline now reliably dated to the late first century. Using a rhetorical style of Jewish origin labelled the *Two Ways,* the *Didache* vividly contrasts the path of "Death and Darkness" with the path of "Life and Light." Focusing on the second Great Commandment, the document features a list of prohibitions that go well beyond the Ten Commandments. Condemnations of theft, murder, and magic appear together with clear denunciations of fornication, adultery, sodomy, infanticide, and abortion. Importantly, the way of Death and Darkness also includes the use of *pharakeia*, or potions. Evil men on this path were "killers of offspring, corrupters of the *plasma* [or mold] of God." In this context, it seems clear that the items being condemned are drugs employed as contraceptives and abortifacients. From the very earliest time, then, the new Christian sexual ethic opposed birth control, alongside other sexual sins.

Linked to this was a fresh sanctification of the marriage bond, involving a radical form of sexual equality. Unlike the Romans and every other ancient culture, the new Christians denounced promiscuity among men as well as women. Paul's exposition in 1 Corinthians 7:2–7 shows a symmetry in conjugal rights that—in the words of historical sociologist Rodney Stark—"was at total variance, not only with pagan culture, but with Jewish culture as well."[137] Reflecting this equality, the average age for first marriage rose to eighteen for Christian women, compared to fourteen with the pagans.

Where the Roman pagans faced a great shortage of fertile females—due to infanticide and botched abortions—the Christian movement had an abundance of young fertile women: an estimated sixty percent of early believers were female. Even after allowing for early practitioners of celibacy, this was a community open to the propagation, protection, and rearing of children.

This openness to procreation had consequences. Although hard numbers on differential fertility do not exist, circumstantial evidence affirms that a novel Christian family and sexual ethic, tied to the abundance of young women, produced a significantly higher number of births and the survival of more offspring to adulthood. Along with conversions (particularly among pagan men married to Christian women), this helps account for the growth in Christian numbers from a negligible figure in 100 A.D. to thirty-two million by A.D. 350, representing half of the empire's population. As Stark concludes, "superior fertility contributed to the rise of Christianity."[138]

Heresies Old . . .

John Noonan was correct in describing how a series of heresies, all hostile to procreation, threatened the young Church. He was incorrect, though, in his claim that the Church's response to these heresies somehow distorted prevailing Christian sexual ethics. These debates worked, instead, to reinforce a set of social doctrines already developed. Noonan also failed to understand that the danger of heretical claims about sexuality was not confined merely to a distant past. Rather, another version of the old darkness was emerging again in the mid-twentieth century. In new guise, it reached a kind of terrible fruition in the 1960s.

The history of the Church's response to such heresies is instructive. The earliest challenge to the life ethic of the young

Christian Church came from the Gnostics, beginning in the first century. Gnosticism emerged independent of Christianity, and drew on a mélange of myths, magic, mysticism, and philosophy. Its central doctrine was a radical dualism, which celebrated the spirit or mind and denigrated the body. The Gnostics rejected the lessons of nature, or natural law. Some entered the Church, and from the inside they argued that the gospel proclaimed by Jesus and Paul liberated them from obedience to any law. They claimed to have a special *gnosis*, or secret knowledge, denied to ordinary Christians.

Regarding family and sexual questions, Gnostics shared two views: they scorned marriage and they detested procreation. Beyond those common beliefs, one strand of Gnosticism emphasized total sexual license. Its ceremonies included ritualized adultery and fornication. This was done, according to one well-documented account from Egypt, "not to beget children, but for mere pleasure." Horrifically, these rituals included perversions of the holy Eucharist, involving menstrual blood and the flesh of aborted babies.[139]

A second Gnostic strand rejected all sexuality. Tatian led a faction labelled the Encratites, or "self-controlled." According to the Church Father Irenaeus, "they attacked marriage as corruption and fornication."[140] Implicitly, they blamed God "for making male and female for the generation of man." In response, they celebrated androgyny. The heretical Gnostic *Gospel of Thomas* has Jesus saying: "Every woman who makes herself male enters the kingdom of heaven."[141]

The epistles carry frequent warnings about Gnostic teachings. In 1 Timothy 4, St. Paul reports that "some will depart from the faith by giving heed to deceitful spirits and doctrines of demons . . . who forbid marriage." Jude 4 warns that entry into the Christian community "has been secretly gained by . . . ungodly persons who pervert the grace of our

God into licentiousness." This Christian defense of procreative marriage from Gnostic assaults would last, in different times and places, for another two centuries.

A second attack on the family ethic of the early Church came from followers of the Iranian prophet Mani (A.D. 216–277). At the apex of his convoluted theology, Mani held that primordial "light" would be liberated by androgynous agents of "the Father," employing lust and abortion. Manichean thought emphasized a firm separation of sex from procreation. The most famous of the followers of Mani was the young Augustine, future bishop of Hippo. Following his conversion to orthodox Christianity, Augustine wrote numerous tracts condemning his old beliefs. From his dialogue, *Against Faustus:*

> For what you most of all detest in marriage is that children be procreated, and so you make your auditors adulterers of their wives when they take care lest the women with whom they copulate conceive.

When the possibility for conception is taken away, Augustine continues, "husbands are the shameful lovers, wives are harlots, wedding beds are stews" and "the bridal chamber a brothel." Other reports have Manicheans employing *coitus interruptus* in rites where the semen is eaten, so as to free a part of God from imprisonment in the human seed.

In the fourth and fifth centuries, Manichaean ideas spread widely within Christian communities. Found again was a renewed celebration of sexual license combined with a hostility to the generation of new human life. Contraception became not only a virtue, but in practice, a sacred act. Again, it took generations of orthodox effort to drive this heresy out of the Church.

Noonan recounts that in the early tenth century a Bulgarian priest named Bogomil resurrected Gnostic radical dualism, centered on opposition to procreation. His ideas spread to Constantinople, and then westward, eventually into France. The heresy effloresced there in the twelfth century, with adherents taking the name of Cathars, or "the Pure." They rejected "the casual works of marriage": "that dirty business which a man does with a woman in carnally mixing with her." For Cathars, "the union of Adam and Eve . . . was forbidden fruit." A woman "conceives in her belly by the cooperation of Satan."[142] The Cathars looked to the disappearance of the human race as the way to set matters right. Cathar practices also appear paradoxically to have sometimes included ritualized fornication (so "to be more swiftly freed from evil nature") and sodomy (the English word "bugger" comes as a derivative of Bulgar). Once again, these anti-marriage, life-changing ideas spread broadly in certain regions. This heresy, too, was finally subdued by the Church's insistence on the necessary linkage of sexual intercourse with procreation.

Importantly, the two great historical schisms in the Christian Church did not involve disagreement of any sort over sexual morality. The eleventh-century break between the Eastern and Western churches occurred over issues of papal authority and the precise nature of the Trinity. The Eastern Orthodox churches would continue to oppose contraception for the near-millennium that followed. The Protestant rebellion of the sixteenth century also involved other issues. As historian Flann Campbell summarizes in the Journal *Population Studies* in 1960:

Even the coming of the Reformation and all it represented in the way of challenge to the dogmas of the medieval

Catholic Church had no influence on Christian doctrine concerning birth control. Protestant divines were as much in agreement on this point as they were in disagreement about others.

Martin Luther deemed marriage to be "the highest order" or calling on Earth, part of the created order. It was "a natural and necessary thing, that whatever is a man must have a woman and whatever is a woman must have a man." He called procreation "the greatest work of God." In his commentary on Genesis, Luther wrote: "Truly in all nature there was no activity more excellent and more admirable than procreation." He linked contraception and abortion to selfishness, adding: "How great, therefore, the wickedness of [fallen] human nature is! How many girls there are who prevent conception and kill and expel tender fetuses, although procreation is the work of God!" After condemning the sin of Onan, Luther added, "Surely at such a time the order of nature established by God in procreation should be followed."[143]

John Calvin concurred: "It is a horrible thing to pour out seed besides the intercourse of man and woman. . . . When a woman in some way drives away the seed out the womb, through aids, then this is rightly seen as an unforgivable crime."[144]

These views would hold firm in every Protestant denomination until 1930. And in every Christian land dominated by Protestants, contraception and abortion also remained illegal.

. . . And Heresies New

Inhabitants of the early twenty-first century have, by and large, learned to live and act within a cultural and social environment that would bewilder, shock, and demoralize a Christian from, say, 1914. Legalized abortion, with millions of babies

lost in "Christian" nations alone each year; a marriage culture
in collapse; astonishingly low fertility rates; half of the few
births that do occur being "without benefit of clergy"; homosexuality and transsexuality idolized and taught to children;
human biology ignored in favor of fifty-seven "genders," each
self-determined; an open sewer of the most graphic and vio-
lent forms of pornography available at a computer click in every home; adultery transformed into a legitimate and lucrative
online business; "Greek love" informally existing as the one
form of child abuse rarely prosecuted (except among clerics);
and contraceptives of an amazing variety publicly subsidized
and even handed out to children.

Writing three decades ago, anthropologist Robin Fox
found that the "accepted" sexual practices of the Roman
Empire held "a range and variety which it has never attained
since."[145] In 2018, the once-Christian nations of the West
have sped well beyond what even the most sex-obsessed Roman pagan could have imagined. To see a world in near-ab-
solute moral and sexual darkness, a contemporary Western
witness need merely open his eyes and look around.

How did this happen? A short answer begins with that
year, 1914, when the Christian nations of Europe and North
America threw themselves into the conflagration then called
the Great War. The slaughterhouses known as the trenches
consumed and maimed millions of men who had believed
in their respective lands, in Christendom, and in God. Such
beliefs were left impaired, or broken. Into the vacuum crept
very old ideas, although in new form.

Indeed, a Christian sexual code nearly two millennia old
faced its most serious challenge since the neo-Gnostic Cathars
threatened human society in the twelfth century. For the first
time in history, wartime governments turned to birth control
devices (condoms) as a way to keep the mobilized sailors and

soldiers disease-free. In the old Russian Empire, the Bolsheviks came to power, complete with a sexual ideology hostile to every aspect of Christian ethics. In Italy and Germany, fascist ideologies claimed to be pro-family, but twisted families and sexuality into servants of imperial conquest. The pseudo-science of sexology emerged in Britain and the United States; its partner was eugenics, which sought to seize procreation from the hands of God and deliver it to men.

At a deeper, more hidden level, the Gnostics also returned, complete with their rejection of nature, the human body, and procreation. Indeed, as found with the Cathars, their agenda became in effect the elimination of humankind. By the 1960s, they were the reputed over-population crisis to cast human beings as a cancer on the planet. Human procreation was once again a disease.

In the first and second Christian centuries, believers found the Church infiltrated by such ideas. The same process occurred in the twentieth. The American experience is illustrative.

Led by Margaret Sanger, founder of the Birth Control League of America, advocates for contraception focused on two strategies: divide the Christians by stoking latent anti-Catholic sentiments among the Protestants and promote eugenics as a means for Protestants to bring on the second coming of Christ.[146]

Prevailing American laws in 1900 conflating and criminalizing contraceptives, abortifacients, and pornography were uniformly the product of Evangelical Protestant fervor, centered on the person of Anthony Comstock, executive secretary of the New York Society for the Suppression of Vice and special agent of the US Postal Service. "Comstock laws" suppressing these matters were on the books in forty-six states, four territories, and at the federal level.

Comstock died in 1915, two years before the whirlwind of moral distortion caused by the Great War hit the United States. Taking his place, somewhat by default, was the Catholic ethicist John A. Ryan. In an important 1916 essay, he reaffirmed the Roman Church's historic condemnation of "all positive means of birth prevention." Why? Because "all these devices constitute the immoral perversion of a human faculty" which had as its "essential end the procreation of offspring."[147] Comstock would have fully agreed.

Sanger, though, skillfully turned the argument in an anti-Catholic direction. Protestants were already worried that the heavy immigration of Catholics from Southern and Eastern Europe threatened the historic Protestant foundations of the land. Ignoring recent history, Sanger leaped on the argument:

> There is no objection to the Catholic Church inculcating its doctrines to its own people, but when it attempts to make these ideas legislative acts and enforce its opinions and code of morals upon the Protestant members of this country, then I do consider its attempt an interference with the principles of this democracy.[148]

With a shrinking number of exceptions, Protestant suspicions regarding the Catholic Church grew in intensity. "Birth control" in Sanger's formulation came to mean liberation from *Catholic* control.

At the same time, many "post-millennial"[149] Protestants came to see eugenics as a means to bring on the kingdom of God. These pastors cast Jesus as the ultimate eugenicist, the "Refiner" of men. One prominent advocate, the Rev. Kenneth MacArthur, explained that "eugenics offers a way, consistent with Christian principles, of freeing the race from the feeble-minded and the criminals," through "surgery or segregation." At the same time, eugenics would encourage "the production of intelligent, healthy, high-minded folk . . . the very material from which to recruit the citizenry of the commonwealth of Christ among men." Such ideas showed "this powerful weapon of birth regulation" to have "great capacities for racial improvement."[150] Most "social gospel" Protestants agreed.

The first Protestant denomination to cast its lot formally with contraception was the Anglican Church. At its famed Lambeth Conference of 1930, and with eugenic ideas lurking just outside the line of direct view, the globe's Anglican bishops, on a vote of 193 to 67 (with forty-six abstaining), approved Resolution Fifteen: "[I]n those cases where there is such a clearly felt moral obligation to limit or avoid parenthood, and where there is a morally sound reason for avoiding complete abstinence, the conference agrees that other methods may be used."

Other Protestant bodies eventually followed. During the 1950s, denominations cheerfully took hold of a phrase developed by the Planned Parenthood Federation of America (as the Birth Control League was now called): "Responsible Parenthood." Under that heading, for example, the Augustana Evangelical Lutheran Church in America endorsed *all* birth control methods within marriage. "None of the methods for controlling the number and spacing of births of children has any special merit or demerit," this church body concluded. Instead, it focused its condemnation on "an unrestrained production of children without realistic regard to God-given responsibilities."[151] The 1958 Anglican Lambeth Conference also declared "responsible parenthood" to be "a right and important factor in Christian family life," with the means of contraception merely "matters of clinical and ascetic choice."[152]

In 1959, the mostly Protestant World Council of Churches issued the *Mansfield Report*. It focused on a "population
explosion" whose repercussions . . . are vast and grave." The
response was still another affirmation of "responsible parenthood," meaning a broad choice of means to "avert or defer
conception."[153]

Conservative Evangelicals in America turned this same
way during the 1960s. The prominent evangelist Billy Graham showed the path when in 1959 he told *The New York
Times* that "there is nothing morally wrong in the practice
of birth control" as a means of controlling the "population
explosion."[154] Fine, even heroic, affirmations of procreative
marriage within the Evangelical press were soon swept away
by fears of an impending "Population Bomb."

The American Evangelical embrace of the new sexual ethic
reached a distorted end in a 1968 conference on "The Control
of Human Reproduction." Jointly sponsored by the lead Evangelical journal *Christianity Today* and the Christian Medical Society, it pulled together a "Who's Who" of Evangelical theologians and leaders. Not only did the group affirm free access
to contraceptives; it also endorsed abortion and sterilization.
Telling was the background paper outlined by medical doctor M.O. Vincent. God's command to "be fruitful and multiply," he said, was "more a blessing than a commandment." The
"overall" lesson from Scripture was that we "all have a *right*
to control conception." Equally symbolic was a paper by the
Wheaton College-educated sociologist John Scanzoni, who
argued that "there are times when it is permissible to snuff out
human life." He concluded: "I am persuaded that the decision
to abort or sterilize is a matter of Christian liberty."

The "Affirmations" of the whole group held to these principles. Over the whole document hung a dark cloud: a malign
condemnation of the 1,900 years of Christian consensus and a

surreal embrace of every form of child denial. Employing language at once arrogant and clear, the "Affirmations" included:

- "The Bible does not expressly prohibit either contraception or abortion."
- "The prevention of conception is not in itself forbidden or sinful."
- "There may be times when a Christian may allow himself (or herself) to be sterilized."
- "[A]bout the necessity and permissibility for [abortion] under certain circumstances we are in accord."
- "This symposium acknowledges the need for Christian involvement in programs of population control at home and abroad."[155]

Significantly, in 1966 the prominent young Evangelical theologian John Warwick Montgomery had argued that Evangelicals could accept birth control "in light of their own physical, emotional, financial, and spiritual situation, and in light of the population picture in their area of the world."[156] And yet, he held still to the humanity of the fetus once conceived, and so opposed abortion. However, in the context of the 1968 consultation, he retreated on this as well, holding that "Christians have no business 'legislating morality'" in a way that would make non-Christians uncomfortable.[157] The Evangelical experience showed that there was no firm ground between an acceptance of contraception and an acceptance of abortion and sterilization. Protestants were feeding into the general darkness falling on the Western world.

A remarkably honest account of what was occurring came from the least likely of sources: the Playboy Press. In 1973, it published a book entitled *The Rape of the APE* [American Puritan Ethic]. It bore three subtitles: *The Official History of the*

Sex Revolution; *The Obscening of America*; and *A RSVP* [Redeeming Social Value Pornography] *Document*. Using bold sarcasm and foul language, it describes how between 1945 and 1973: "Legions of Lolitas joined the battle with battalions of Babbitts and platoons of Portnoys. Manners and morals and great institutions bit the dust. Waterbeds splashed, and vibrators jiggled." In the end, "No one knew exactly how, but Western civilization had been caught with its pants down."

This book focused on the United States, but there were similar developments in other Western lands. *The Rape of the APE* tells how a group of men coming of age in the 1940s and "dirty-minded beyond belief" set out "to defile the world's most antiseptic culture and corrupt the world's most respectable citizenry." Tactics would be harsh:

Wherever there was a Strawberry Church Social, they would search and destroy. They would storm every bastion of decency; besmirch and defile the Enemy on the beaches, in the homes and in the streets. They would recruit allies among the corrupt, and despoil the innocent.

Of high importance, they would also open new "sex fronts": "science, for example. They would give smut respectability by dressing it in the dignified cloak of science." Of highest importance, they would also need "to get God off" the side of purity and virtue.

The book gives a blow-by-blow account of how these "dirty-minded" figures won every cultural, social, and legal battle they entered, including the surrender of most Protestant churches. In the process,

Everything got devalued. Not just the dollar but everything in American life. The American Flag was devalued.

Marriage was devalued. Virginity. Love. God. Mother-hood. Mom's Apple Pie. General Motors has less value now, and so does the Bill of Rights.

The Playboy Press volume continues:

The quality of men available to lead was devalued. Our . . . institutions and our customs were devalued; the worth of an individual was devalued. All the Pleasures were devalued. [Sexual intercourse] too. Especially too.[158]

Darkness Descends on Rome

This fair accounting of the tactics, consequences, and human and sexual casualties of the new darkness spreading over the globe frames the Catholic debate over birth control during the 1960s. Back in 1930, Pope Pius XI had responded to the Anglican approval of contraception within marriage by issuing the encyclical *Casti Connubii,* which reaffirmed the historic Christian consensus: "Since . . . the conjugal act is destined primarily by nature for the begetting of children, those who in exercising it deliberately frustrate its natural power and purpose, sin against nature and commit a deed which is shameful and intrinsically vicious."

Pius did, though, give a blessing to sexual abstinence during a women's fertile period for serious reasons. Aware, it appears, of the use by some Protestants and the secular intelligentsia of eugenic arguments to justify birth control, Pius XI also used this encyclical to condemn eugenic sterilizations. He reasoned, "Those who act in this way are at fault in losing sight of the fact that the family is more sacred than the state and that men are begotten not for the earth and for time, but for heaven and eternity."[159]

In 1961, the issue of birth control reopened in Vatican circles. Theologians wrote journal articles questioning components of Pius XI's arguments. At the popular level, the Catholic physician John Rock—one of the inventors of the progestin contraceptive pill—argued in *Good Housekeeping* that this new method of regulating births was actually in line with Catholic teaching. The synthetic hormone in the pill, he said, merely allowed humans to use their reason to do predictably what nature did in an unpredictable manner.

The same year, Pope John XXIII issued his call to convene a great Vatican Council, so "that the sacred heritage of Christian truth be safeguarded and expounded with greater efficacy." The pope also created the Pontifical Commission for the Study of Population, Family and Births. Cardinal Leo Suenens of Belgium, reporting later that he had advised the pope to create the commission, says he told Pope John that it was time for "an intelligent position on responsible parenthood and at least try to reform the old idea, the more children the better." Protestants from that era would recognize the phrasing.

Following the death of John and the ascension of Paul VI to the throne of St. Peter, the pontifical commission went on a wild ride: greatly expanding its membership and reorganizing several times, and facing growing pressure to accept at least "the pill" as in line with the natural law. By 1965, a clear majority of the theologians, physicians, and laymen on the panel were in favor of reversing the Church's historical position and the categorical condemnation of contraception presented in *Casti Connubii,* and allowing the "anovulant pill" in certain cases for married couples.

The pope was torn on how to proceed. "So many problems!" he told an interviewer in 1965. "Take birth control, for example. The world asks what we think, and we find

ourselves trying to give an answer. But what answer? . . .
We have to say something. But what? God will simply have
to enlighten us."[160]

A year later, in another interview, Paul worried that
"[a]ny attenuation of the law [regarding birth control] would
have the effect of calling morality into question . . . Theology would then become the servant of science . . . science's
handmaid." A new scientific discovery might come along,
he said, "where we would have to admit procreation without a father; the whole moral edifice would collapse."

He also presciently asked whether another consequence
of accepting contraception might be "that the pill may produce monsters in the next generation." Indeed, as we will
see later, it appears that the pill is altering the human genetic
inheritance not so much to produce monsters, but to produce less masculine men, even as it has incentivized a great
deal of monstrous behavior of men toward women.

Like a small cavalry riding under the banner of the cross,
a cadre of men came to his aid. Leading them was Cardinal Alfredo Ottaviani, pro-prefect of the Congregation for
the Doctrine of the Faith. His detractors described him as
"multi-jowled and almost completely blind, stubborn, demanding, imperious, suspicious, ill at ease with the press—
the unconditional reactionary."[161] He actually held a keen
sense that the whole of the natural law rested at this moment on a defense of Christian sexual ethics. He, in turn,
summoned two American theologians to his side: the Je-
suit monsignor John C. Ford, professor of moral theology
at the Catholic University of America and co-author of the
monumental *Contemporary Moral Theology;* and the young lay
theologian Germain Gabriel Grisez, an associate professor of
philosophy at Georgetown University and author of *Contraception and the Natural Law* (1964).

In June 1966, those seeking a break with *Casti Con-nubii* and all that came before leaked to certain carefully selected progressive Catholic press outlets, against Pope Paul's wishes, three of the documents presented to Pope Paul during the commission's deliberations, billing them (improperly) as the "Majority Report." Predictably titled "Schema for a Document on Responsible Parenthood," the primary document was an encomium to moral change. It celebrated a world that "always undergoes change" and "man's tremendous progress in control of matter by technological means." The document held that "it is natural to man to use his skill in order to put under human control of what is given by physical nature." Other stirring signs of an unprecedented new age were "changes in the role of the woman," "new bodies of knowledge in biology, psychology, sexuality, and demography," and "a better, deeper, and *more correct* understanding of conjugal life" (emphasis added).

Embracing the historical arguments of John Noonan, the so-called Majority Report held that Christian opposition to heresies over 1,200 years had warped doctrine: "Nor was there maintained always a right equilibrium of all the elements." In certain cases, the use of contraception, they held, would "foster a spirituality which is more profound in married life" and would also lead to "the genuine fostering of all families in a context of *social evolution* which should be truly human" (emphasis added).[162]

One of the other leaked documents, presented as an appendix to the Majority Report, was authored by Monsignor Ford and Professor Grisez, and labeled (again, inaccurately) as the "Minority Report." In what was actually just one of several documents presented to Pope Paul VI, they offered a defense of the natural law as understood for 1,900 years and the recognition that a dark force—one seen before—was descending on and disrupting the Christian world.

In this advisory document, as with others presented to Pope Paul, Ford and Grisez were adamant that the Church's unbroken condemnation of contraception was not the consequence of historical distortions:

> Why did the Church always teach this doctrine? Not as a reaction against . . . heresies, not because the Fathers . . . accepted the Stoic philosophy, not because . . . they followed some philosophy of nature which is now obsolete.

Instead, "because, reflecting on the scriptures and what they found there about the nature of human life and the nature of Christian chastity, they saw that contraception was a *violation* of human life and Christian chastity." Forged in the first century, this was—contra the proposal from the innovators—"the truly new morality," grounded in natural law, and not open to change.

The example of contemporary Protestant churches loomed large for them. These "separated brethren," in accepting contraception, had already made themselves "irrelevant" to the world on major moral questions. Having denied Christian doctrine on the marital act, they "progressively and inevitably" turned to even greater "denials of the norms of Christian chastity," including abortion. Having abandoned "the new morality of Christ," Protestants found themselves absorbed by the new "morality of the times." Ford and Grisez predicted that other deviations would quickly follow, including assent to extramarital and premarital sex and homosexuality. Indeed, as they asked [in the year 1968!], "if the life-giving and love-giving meanings of sexual intercourse are not inseparably linked, could not one man 'marry' another man—always with true love-giving intent—or one woman, another woman?"[163]

The two theologians, moreover, saw an even darker cloud falling: a return of the anti-life Gnostics. "Contraception springs from a will turned against the beginning of a new human life," they said. Or as reformulated, "the will to prevent conception is a will turned against human life in advance." Referring to St. Paul, they noted that "[t]he world of today sometimes reminds [us] of the pagan world of which he was speaking." Specifically, the Majority Report exhibited an ambivalence toward the human body. Christian doctrine held that "[m]an is an integral whole; the human person *is* a body." Put another way, a "man's biology is part of his personality. Men are not angelic creatures, spirits without bodies."

The Majority Report, however, tended to a "dualism," casting the body "as a mere biological datum," made operational only by man's dominion. Ford and Grisez responded: "This ambivalence is strikingly similar to the attitude toward the human body and human sexuality one finds in agnosticism, Manichaeism, and Catharism."[164]

This attitude fed into the view that human life was "a mere product of human ingenuity"; some would-be reformers even spoke of "changing human nature." The Christian view, they countered, held reverence for the human body pure and inviolate, "for this body will rise again, and is destined to live forever with Christ."

Ford and Grisez also forcefully rejected the argument that the oral contraceptive pill had somehow changed the moral framework for debate regarding human sexuality. "It has become clear that the new methods have the same moral significance as the old."[165]

They concluded that "[t]his Christian morality, firmly anchored in divine teachings expressed in Holy Writ, is a lifeline which saves those who hold fast to it as they struggle through the torrent of life." The rejection of contraception also served as "the first line of defense in the protection which surrounds what is sacred and inviolable—innocent human life."[166] The precept found in *Casti Connubii* "is as valid today as it was yesterday, and it will be the same tomorrow and always," because it is "the expression of a law which is natural and divine." Taught by the apostles during the first Christian century, "in a world where few appreciated this virtue," it would soon serve as "a prime contribution of Catholicism to a future reintegrated Christianity."[167]

Prophecies, Woefully Fulfilled

Paul VI issued *Humanae Vitae* on July 25, 1968. It reaffirmed *Casti Connubii*, most notably in section eleven: "The Church . . . in urging men to the observance of the precepts of the natural law, which it interprets by its constant doctrine, teaches that each and every marital act must of necessity retain its intrinsic relationship to the procreation of human life." The encyclical also contained certain prophecies:

- Widespread use of contraception would "lead to conjugal infidelity and the general lowering of morality."

- The contracepting "man" would lose respect for "the woman" and no longer look to "her physical and psychological equilibrium," even viewing her "as a mere instrument of selfish enjoyment."

- Widespread contraception would place "a dangerous weapon in the hands of those public authorities who take no heed of moral exigencies."

- Reflecting the new Gnosticism, man would believe that he had an unlimited dominion over his body.

How well have these prophecies held up? Consider the following research results offered by medical researchers, economists, psychologists, sociologists, and social biologists.

- Using a large American sample, a 2015 study on the relationship between divorce and the use of oral contraceptives, sterilization, and abortion, found that these practices "increased the likelihood of divorce—up to two times," when compared to couples using Natural Family Planning. Researcher Richard Fehring draws the inevitable inference: "Contraceptive use, sterilization, and abortion seem to have a destructive effect on the marital bond." Why? Pointing to the oral contraceptive, he notes that "the female brain is a major receiver of the synthetic hormonal steroids" found in the pill. These "have structural effects on regions of the brain that govern higher-order cognitive activities, suggesting that a woman on birth control pills may literally not be herself—or is herself, on steroids." These neurological effects may "help explain marital dynamics that lead to divorce."[168]

- This confirms the earlier speculations of Rutgers University sociobiologist Lionel Tiger, who held, "It is impossible to overestimate the impact of the contraceptive pill on human arrangements." There are no other examples, he said, even close to the pill, of a "powerful drug provided daily to healthy people that affects such a fundamental element of human life." Among the effects are: a broad depression in male sperm counts, as a consequence of millions of women mimicking pregnancy through use of the pill; a diminished romantic interest by men in women; a change in the way contracepting women relate to non-contracepting women; a sharp decline in the responsibility felt by men toward their sexual partners, married or not; and a general breakdown in natural human mating patterns. Tiger concludes that "[n]othing less changed than *all* the central mechanism of sexual selection, which [had] produced the sexual system that prompted people to engage in it at all" (emphasis added). Meanwhile the contemporaneous turn to widespread sterilization showed a "not-so-hidden nihilism about reproduction."[169]

- In an article that sent shockwaves when it appeared in 1996, Nobel laureate in economics George Akerlof and his wife, future Federal Reserve chair Janet Yellen, joined with Michael Katz to show that legalized contraception and abortion were the primary causes of a surge in out-of-wedlock childbearing in the United States. In this new era, the "shotgun wedding" of a pregnant young woman to her lover disappeared. Men could now assume that a new sexual partner was on the pill; if not, the law gave her the sole choice to have an abortion. In practice, men were freed from age-old obligations.

  As the authors summarize: "The sexual revolution, by making the birth of the child the *physical* choice of the mother, makes child support a *social* choice of the father" (emphasis added). Put in economic terms, "the availability of female contraception" brought "a decline in the competitive position of women relative to men." More specifically, who were the losers in this moral and social scramble? The authors answer: "women who want children" and "women who, because of . . . religious conviction, have failed to adopt the new innovations." Indeed, those females who wanted to marry and bear children were "immiserated." Meanwhile, "there are fewer men willing to get married." Why? A "decline in intimacy between [short term] sexual partners" simply reinforces "the unwillingness to marry."[170]

• In an equally remarkable study of mate choice among humans, a 2009 article in *Trends in Ecology and Evolution* shows how contraceptives have profoundly affected the most basic of male-female relations. Pill users, for example, are less attracted to masculine men. Men find pill-using women significantly less attractive, as well. Summarized: "The contraceptive pill appears to interfere with natural mate preferences." Although the long-term effects are still unknown, the authors speculate that "if pill users mate with less masculine men and masculinity is heritable, then their children are also likely to express less masculine phenotypes." Meanwhile, "marital dissatisfaction owing to the effect of the pill on mate choice could [negatively] influence the duration and stability of long-term relationships." Alas, even the evolutionists are now deeply worried.[171]

• In its social teachings, the Catholic Church has consistently celebrated and defended the full-time mother in the home. As Pope St. John Paul II wrote in his 1981 apostolic exhortation *Familiaris Consortio*, "society must be structured in such a way that wives and mothers are not in practice compelled to work outside the home." In his encyclical *On Human Work* he also insists that a family-sustaining wage be paid to fathers, a matter serving as "a concrete means of verifying the justice of the whole socio-economic system involved." The contraceptive revolution tore through these aspirations. As a paper published by the National Bureau of Economic Research in 2000 concludes, "[t]he pill had a direct positive effect on women's career investment by almost eliminating the chance of becoming pregnant and thus the cost of having sex." This, in turn, has discouraged early marriage, encouraged young women to invest in careers rather than in family formation, and substantially reduced their lifetime fertility. These are among the fruits of what the authors approvingly refer to as "the power of the pill."[172]

- A new literature review in the fields of psychology, sociology, and the scientific study of religion found similar results. The availability of hormonal contraception facilitated the separation of sex from procreation, encouraged women to extend their education or enter careers, delayed childbirth, encouraged cohabitation, and supported a turn to non-procreative intercourse. The researchers conclude: "This freedom has also led to fewer or later marriages, more divorce, low sexual desire, and depression. For those whose religion proscribes the use of contraceptives, it has often led to diminished religious practice."[173]

- Finally, historian Matthew Connelly documents in his book *Fatal Misconception: The Struggle to Control World Population* the ways in which protagonists "did, in fact, act in underhanded ways, pretending their organizations were dedicated to one agenda while secretly harboring another." The "wartime-type approach" to population control adopted by leading foundations, United Nations agencies, and the like included forced sterilizations, coerced abortions, and penalties for child birth, the very sort of governmental "weapons" foreseen by Paul VI in HV.[174]

Few Christian documents can claim such resounding secular and scientific affirmation.

Shortly after the promulgation of HV, and in the midst of a gale of protests by Catholics and non-Catholics alike, Paul VI told his friend Cardinal Edward Gagnon: "Don't be afraid; in twenty years' time they'll call me a prophet."[175] He was right, of course; although fifty years later, this is even more certainly true.

Indeed, the historical legacy of HV is now clear. Almost alone at the time, Paul VI perceived a moral darkness descending on the globe, a new Gnosticism emerging after being dormant for 800 years, complete with its old campaigns against human nature and human life.

In response, Pope Paul thrust the banner of Christian truth in the soil before the surging juggernaut of the sexual revolution. If he did not stop it cold, he did confuse, disorient, and disrupt the charge. If there had been no *Humanae Vitae*, or if the papacy had issued a document based on the Majority Report, all would have been lost. The revolution would have triumphed universally. Abortion and sterilization, just like contraception, would have become positive universal human rights everywhere. Transsexuality, gender theory, and other subsequent and deadly fantasies would have become firmly fixed in the laws of nations. Paul VI understood that the prohibition of artificial contraception was the fundamental barrier. If one compromised on that, all other defenses would have crumbled.

Finally, HV created time and space for pro-life and pro-family movements to emerge and confront the darkness. Without the encyclical on human life, Evangelicals would have consummated their embrace of abortion, sterilization, and population control. With it, conditions and guilty consciences allowed reassertion of pro-life sentiments among conservative Protestants during the 1970s, and even a subsequent new questioning of birth control. More directly, HV gave encouragement and new vigor to an array of Catholic pro-life and pro-family groups, many of which might have never come into existence without its witness.

It also bought time for the Eastern Orthodox churches, particularly those under the thumb of Communism in 1968. With the fall of that ideology in the early 1990s, Orthodox religious leaders recovered their bearings. Indeed, in 2018, the Eastern churches and their patriarchs have become leaders in the global fight for life, family, and human fertility. As John Ford and Germain Grisez had predicted, the message of *Humanae Vitae* has become "a prime contribution of Catholicism" to a reintegrating Christianity.

Whatever might happen in the future, such achievements cannot be taken away. As in the first Christian century, life and light had again appeared, guiding our way on that path into the next fifty years.

~

Joseph C. Atkinson, S.T.D. is associate professor of Sacred Scripture at the John Paul II Institute at the Catholic University of America in Washington, D.C. He is a leading expert in the biblical and theological foundations of the family and has done extensive and groundbreaking research on the family's role in salvation history. He is the author of *Biblical and Theological Foundations of the Family: The Domestic Church* (CUA Press, 2014) and founder of the Theology of the Family Project (TheologyOfTheFamily.com). He and his wife, Nancy, have been married thirty-eight years and have six children.

Paul Gondreau, S.T.D. is professor of theology at Providence College in Rhode Island. He is the author of numerous scholarly works on marriage and human sexuality and on Christology, including essays in various collections and in such scholarly journals as *Nova et Vetera* and *The Thomist,* with particular specialization in the thought of St. Thomas Aquinas. He was formerly a consultant to the United States Conference of Catholic Bishops' committee on Laity, Marriage, Family, and Youth.

Mark S. Latkovic, S.T.D. is professor of moral theology at Sacred Heart Major Seminary in Detroit, where he has taught since 1990. Among his many popular and scholarly publications are *What's a Person to Do? Everyday Decisions that Matter* (OSV, 2013) and (as co-editor) *St. Thomas Aquinas and the Natural Law Tradition: Contemporary Perspectives* (CUA Press, 2004). Married for more than thirty years, he and his wife have four children and one grandchild.

Shaun and Jessica McAfee are converts to the Catholic Church. Shaun is the author of *Reform Yourself! How to Pray, Find Peace, and Grow in Faith with the Saints of the Counter-Reformation* (Catholic Answers Press) and other books. He blogs at the National Catholic Register and founded EpicPew.com. Jessica is a FertilityCare Practitioner for the Pope Paul VI Institute and contributes to many online resources. They have four children and live in Vicenza, Italy.

Allan Carlson, Ph.D. is the author of fifteen books and hundreds of articles on family questions, including most recently *Family Cycles: Strength, Decline & Renewal in American Domestic Life, 1630-2000* (Transaction, 2016). He is currently the John Howard Distinguished Senior Fellow at the International Organization for the Family.

Stephen Phelan is vice president of family initiatives for the St. John Paul II Foundation in Houston, where he oversees the foundation's *Together in Holiness* conference and education efforts. After earning a master's degree in philosophy at Franciscan University, he served as director of communications for Human Life International for nine years. He and his wife, Dianne, live in Katy, Texas, with their three children.

Todd Aglialoro is director of publishing for Catholic Answers. He holds a master's degree from the International Theological Institute for Studies on Marriage and the Family. He and his wife have seven children and reside in the San Diego area.

1 "Hac de causa S. Synodus, dum instantissime omnes hortatur ut quisque pro sua possibilitate familias numerosas efficaciter adiuvet, simul severe reprobat commendationem vel propagationem inhonestorum mediorum anticonceptionalium ad delimitandam prolem; quibus non tantum non defenditur bonum populorum, ut hodie aliquando praetenditur, sed potius corrumpitur totus ordo socialis." *Acta et Documenta Concilio Oecumenico Vaticano II Apparando*, Series II (Praeparatoria), Vol. III, Acta Commissionum et Secretariatuum Praeparatoriorum Concilii Oecumenici Vaticani II, Pars I (Città del Vaticano: Typis Polyglottis Vaticanis, 1969), p. 130, n. 34.

2 Cf. Can. 1752.

3 Cf. *Humanae Vitae* 17.

4 Cf. *Evangelium Vitae* 97.

5 "*ut progressionis prorsus humana significatio describatur, quam Ecclesia proponit.*"

6 "Litterae encyclicae «*Humanae vitae*» *solida vincula* designant, *quae inter vitae ethicam et ethicam socialem intercedunt*, magistrale quoddam insinuantes argumentum, quod gradatim variis in documentis auctum est, novissime in Ioannis Pauli II Litteris encyclicis *Evangelium vitae.*"

7 "*Ecclesia, cui cordi est verus hominis progressus, monet eum ad plenam valorum observantiam, in sexualitate quoque exercenda: quae ad meram rem hedonisticam ludicramque redigi non potest, sicut educatio sexualis in technicam institutionem coartari non potest, si tantum cura habeatur eos quorum interest arcendi a quodam contagio vel a generandi «periculo». Hoc modo pauperior fieret et altus sexualitatis sensus extenuaretur, qui econtra agnosci et accipi debet cum responsalitate tam singularum personarum quam communitatis.*"

8 "*novis generationibus adhuc proponendi pulchritudinem familiae et matrimonii, congruentiam huiusmodi institutionum cum altioribus postulatis cordis dignitatisque personae.*"

9   "*Status vocantur ad normas politicas edendas, praeeminentiam integ-
     ritatemque familiae promoventes, quae matrimonio nititur unius viri
     uniusque mulieris, quaeque exstat prima vitalisque societatis cellula,
     atque in se recipit etiam quaestiones oeconomicas et nummarias, quod
     ad ipsius necessitudinis indolem attinet.*"

10   "umile e profetica testimonianza di amore a Cristo e alla
     sua Chiesa." Franciscus PP, Homilia "Episcoporum Synodi
     Conventu Extraordinario exitum habente necnon occasione
     beatificationis Pauli VI Papae," 19 Octobris 2014, *Acta Apos-
     tolicae Sedis* 106 (2014), 825. English translation: "Homily for
     the Beatification of Giovanni Battista Montini," *L'Osservatore
     Romano*, Weekly Edition in English, 24 October 2014, p. 9.

11   *Westminster Confession of Faith (1647)*, Article 1.7

12   See Babylonian Talmud, *Shabbath* 17 b.

13   http://www.amislejeune.org/index.php/en/jerome-lejeune/
     jerome-lejeunes-message/conferences/adam-et-eve-ou-le-
     monogenisme accessed February 22, 2018.

14   Court testimony of Jerome Lejeune given in February 1992 in
     Davis vs. Davis, Blount County, TN: Accessed at http://www.
     sedin.org/propeng/embryos.htm on February 23, 2018.

15   See Bryan Hodge, *The Christian Case against Contraception* (Eugene,
     OR: Wipf & Stock, 2010,) 28-38; C. Provan, The Bible and Birth
     Control (*Monongahela, PA* Zimmer Printing, 1989), 62-97.

16   See *Creation vs Chaos*, Bernhard Anderson (Eugene, OR: Wipf
     & Stock, 2005), 111-112.

17   C. Westermann, *Genesis 1-11*, trans. J. Scullion (Minneapolis,
     MN: Fortress Press, 1994), 65.

18   J. Prichard, *Ancient Near Eastern Text*, 2nd ed. (Princeton, NJ:
     Princeton University Press, 1955) 61, line 6ff; 120 b.

19   M. Kaufman, *Love, Marriage, and Family in Jewish Law and Tradition*
     (Northvale, NJ: Jason Aronson, 1992) 139 (emphasis in original).

20   Shulhan Aruch, Even HaEzer 1:1, cited by Kaufman, *Marriage.
     Love, and Family*, 5.

21   These are two different orders and so there is no reading back
     of sexuality into the Godhead. Also, this iconic function is
     in embryonic form in these texts but develops organically

throughout history.

22 Without knowing the end (*telos*) of a human act, no proper moral evaluation can be made.

23 See J. Atkinson, *Biblical and Theological Foundations of the Family* (Washington, DC: CUA Press, 2014), 148-160.

24 See S. Hirsch, *The Pentateuch/Leviticus (part II)* 2nd ed. trans. I. Levy (Gateshead, England: Judaica Press, 1976), 584.

25 Kaufmann, *Love, Marriage and Family*, 116.

26 Mary Douglas, *Purity and Danger*, (New York: Routledge & Kegan Paul, 2005), 67.

27 Christine A. McCann, *Transgressing the Boundaries of Holiness* (Seton Hall University eRepository @ Seton Hall, 2010) 4, emphasis added. Accessed March 8, 2018. http://scholarship. shu.edu/cgi/viewcontent.cgi?article=1076&context=theses.

28 One should conceive of contraceptive behavior as a societal ritual. To understand its meaning, one would have to identify the over-arching value upon which that society was formed.

29 See Jacob Milgrom, *Leviticus 1-16* (New York: Doubleday, 1991), 732.

30 This is illustrated in 2 Samuel 6 where Uzzah dies when he touched the Ark. Only the sons of Aaron (i.e., priests) were allowed to touch the *sancta* of the Temple. Uzzah appears not to have been a priest with the proper status of holiness, and so in touching the Ark, he effected a clash between conflicting spheres and dies.

31 Kaufman, *Marriage, Love, and Family*, 197.

32 This and all Talmudic references are taken from the online William Davidson Talmud at https://www.sefaria.org/ william-davidson-talmud. Accessed February 24-25, 2018.

33 A fuller explanation of this is given in J. Pedersen, *Israel Its Life and Culture I-II* ((London: Oxford University Press, 1926; reprint, 1954), 109. See Atkinson, *Biblical and Theological Foundations*, 161-196.

34 See Niddah 13a. The rabbinical teaching on male contraception comes directly from the understanding of scriptural texts. In general, rabbis make allowance for female contraceptive

behavior in certain situations, but this is not based *on biblical texts* but on the Talmudic story of the Beraita of the Three Women (see *Yebamoth* 12b). "The Babylonian Talmud states . . . that real holiness comes from rabbinic law, not biblical law." *Hermeneutics of Holiness: Ancient Jewish and Christian Notions of Sexuality*, Naomi Koltun-Fromm (New York: Oxford University Press, 2010), 225. This is a critical distinction; in our essay, we are only dealing with biblical teachings.

35   See *Shulchan Aruch*, *Even HaEzer* 23:5.

36   Romans 1:25 literally reads: "they exchanged the truth about God for the lie." This would seem to be a midrash on the Fall in Genesis 3.

37   See Pedersen, *Israel*, 99; H. Wheeler Robinson. "The Hebrew Conception of Corporate Personality," *Werden und Wesen des Alten Testaments, B.Z.A.W.* 66 (1936).

38   St. Irenaeus, on the gnostic Carpocrates: "They declare they have in their power all things which are irreligious and impious, and are at liberty to practise them" *Against Heresies Book 1*, Ch. 25, 4. Accessed on March 15, 2018 at http://www.newadvent.org/fathers/0103125.htm.

39   H.B. von Balthasar, *"A Word on 'Humanae Vitae'"* in *Christian Married Love* (San Francisco, CA: Ignatius Press, 1981) 56.

40   A. Villeneuve expresses something similarly when he writes: "Yet unity finds its fullest and strongest expression in the language of love . . . and most especially in the metaphor of the "one-flesh" union in marriage This theme regroups together all of the aforementioned ones, namely, the consecration of the Church/Temple/bride for the purpose of sanctification, rooted in a permanent covenantal bond of love, and fully expressed in humble self-sacrifice. *Nuptial Symbolism in the Second Temple Writing, the New Testament, and Rabbinic Writings* (Boston, MA: Brill, 2016), 220.

41   Andrew Lincoln in his commentary on Ephesians uses two descriptors that show the depth of this comparison. He says it is both "the standard and *prototype* for the writer's instructions about human marriage," and "the *archetype* for human marriage,

the one-flesh relationship between husband and wife" *Ephesians*, (Nashville, TX: Thomas Nelson, 1990) 352, 362.

42   Andre Villeneuve, *Nuptial Symbolism Nuptial Symbolism*, 232.

43   10:8.

44   Clement of Alexandria, *Christ the Educator*, Book 2:10 in *The Fathers of the Church Series*, trans. Simon Wood, Vol. 23 (Washington, DC: CUA Press, 2008), 173.

45   *The Refutation of All Heresies*, Book 9:7, Trans. J.H. MacMahon (Edinburg: T&T Clark, 1868), 345.

46   Fathers of the Church Series, Vol. 20, (Washington, DC: CUA Press) quoted by John Harvey, *The Catholic Tradition on the Morality of Contraception*, http://www.therealpresence.org/archives/Abortion_Euthanasia/Abortion_Euthanasia_004.htm accessed March 12, 2018.

47   *Letters of St. Jerome*, in Ancient Church Writers, Vol. 1, trans. C. Mierow, (New York: Paulist Press, 1963), 145.

48   John Chrysostom, *Homilies on The Gospel of Matthew* (28:5), quoted by John Hardon, *Contraception* (ibid.)

49   St. Caesarius of Arles, *Sermons (51), Volume 1*, trans. M. M. Mueller, in *The Fathers of the Church Series*, Vol. 31 (Washington, DC: CUA Press, 1956), 259.

50   Augustine, *Treatises on Marriage and Other Subjects* in *The Fathers of the Church Series*, Vol. 27, trans. Charles Huegelmeyer, (Washington, DC: CUA Press, 1955) 116-117. See also *De Conjugiis Adulterinis* 2, 12; CSEL 41, 396 and Bryan C. Hodge, *The Christian Case Against Contraception* (Eugene, OR: Wipf & Stock, 2010), 68-72.

51   Quoted by J. Noonan, *Contraception: A History Of Its Treatment By Catholic Theologians And Canonists* (Cambridge, MA: Harvard University Press, 1965), 168.

52   Noonan, *Contraception*, 155-161.

53   *Luther's Works*, Vol 7: *Lectures on Genesis 38-44*, trans. Paul D. Pahl (St. Louis, MO: Concordia Publishing House, 1965) Ch. 38, 20-21.

54   John Calvin, *Commentary on the First Book of Moses called Genesis*, Vol. 2, (Gen. 38:8-10), trans. John King in Christian Classics

Ethereal Library, (print basis Grand Rapids, MI: Baker, 1996), 184.

55 These parts of the DNA are God as the author of conception and life, the order of creation, the Onan incident, the holiness of God, and the participation of marriage and therefore sexual union in the salvific work of Christ.

56 See Introduction to *Majority Report of the Papal Commission for the Study of Problems of the Family, Population, and Birth Rate*: "The story of God and of man, therefore, should be seen that man's tremendous progress in control of matter by technical means," accessed March 15, 2018 at http://www.bostonleadershipbuilders.com/0church/birth-control-majority.htm.

57 It must be noted that Georges Cardinal Cottier, theologian of the pontifical household under John Paul II and a friend of the Swiss Dominican who was the secretary of that commission, acknowledged in an interview near the end of his life that the commission members lacked an adequate grasp of the science of contraception; they thought, for instance, that the birth control pill acted not as a block of the natural process, but as a kind of medication that "helped nature" by prolonging the woman's natural period of infertility.

58 See Patrice Favre, *Georges Cottier. Itinéraire d'un croyant* (Tours, France: Éditions CLD, 2007), 188-192.

59 Vatican Information Service, "Family, Dialogue, New Evangelization: Central Themes of Benedict XVI's Address to the Roman Curia," December 21, 2012; www.vatican.va.

60 Vatican Information Service (Benedict XVI), "Blessed are the Peacemakers," 4; December 14, 2012; www.vatican.va.

61 The citations are from Julia Meloni, "The Man Who Was 'Ante-Pope,'" *Crisis Magazine*, February 28, 2018 (www.crisismagazine.com); here she is speaking of and citing Cardinal Carlo Martini of Milan, based on his and Georg Sporschill's *Night Conversations with Cardinal Martini: The Relevance of the Church for Tomorrow* (New York: Paulist Press, 2012).

62 Mary Eberstadt, "The Prophetic Power of *Humanae Vitae*: Documenting the Realities of the Sexual Revolution," *First Things*, April, 2018; accessible online at www.firsthings.

com. In this essay, Eberstadt "count[s] up the new realities vindicating *Humanae Vitae*, one by one."

63 *Paradiso*, Canto XIV, trans. Anthony Esolen (New York: Modern Library, 2004), 147.

64 *Summa Theologiae* I:91:3.

65 René Descartes, *A Discourse on the Method of Correctly Conducting One's Reason and Seeking Truth in the Sciences*, Part 4; trans. Ian Maclean (Oxford: University of Oxford Press, 2006), 29. The fuller passage in which this statement appears reads: "I thereby concluded that I was a *substance* whose whole *essence* or nature resides only in thinking, and which, in order to exist, has no need of place and is not dependent on any material thing. Accordingly this 'I', that is to say, the soul by which I am what I am, is entirely distinct from the body and is even easier to know than the body; and would not stop being everything it is, even if the body were not to exist."

66 *Phaedo*, 80-1.

67 Wendell Berry, "Feminism, the Body, and the Machine," in *What Are People for? Essays by Wendell Berry* (New York: North Point Press, 1990), 178-96, at 190.

68 Descartes, *A Discourse on the Method*, Part 6 (trans. Maclean, 51).

69 This director was the plastic surgeon John Hoopes, as reported by Laura Wexler, "Identity Crisis," *Baltimore Style*, January-February, 2007 (www.baltimorestyle.com).

70 This is from the Catholic priest and sociologist/novelist, Andrew Greeley, *Sex: The Catholic Experience* (Allen, Texas: Thomas More, 1994), 75 and 82.

71 The former comes from Richard McCormick, "The Consistent Ethic of Life: Is There a Historical Soft Underbelly?", in *The Critical Calling* (Washington, DC: Georgetown University Press, 1989), 211-32 (cited in Romanus Cessario, *Introduction to Moral Theology* [Washington, DC: Catholic University of America Press, 2001], 72, n. 50); the latter is from Philip S. Keane, *Sexual Morality: A Catholic Perspective* (New York: Paulist Press, 1977), 46.

72 For the first citation, James Alison, "From Impossibility to

Responsibility: Developing New Narratives for Gay Catholic Living" (originally a talk delivered to the Georgetown University LGBTQ Center on January 27, 2010, and subsequently posted on his website, www.jamesalison.co.uk). The second citation comes from the psychotherapist and moral theologian Daniel A. Helminiak, *Sex and the Sacred: Gay Identity and Spiritual Growth* (New York: Harrington Park Press, 2006), 92-3; here Helminiak also writes: "Psychological studies show that the *distinctive* function of human sex is intimacy and relationship, not procreation." Emphasis his.

73   Thus, Jean Porter, "Natural Law and Innovative Forms of Marriage: A Reconsideration," *Journal of the Society of Christian Ethics* 30.2 (2010), 79-97, at 93: "if the sexual function can credibly be seen as serving other natural purposes [than the procreative one], then arguably, *these can legitimately be pursued independently of one another,* even through sexual acts that are structurally or deliberately nonprocreative" (emphasis mine). Porter has in mind same-sex unions as an example of a sexual act that is "structurally nonprocreative," and contraception marks an obvious example of one that is "deliberately nonprocreative." It is noteworthy that in an article that draws upon the natural-law doctrine of the thirteenth-century, Porter offers but one brief reference to Aquinas, and instead uses as her main authority Philip the Chancellor's *Summa de Bono.* For good reason does she leave Aquinas on the sideline in her natural-law pitch for same-sex unions! If Porter distinguishes in order to separate, Aquinas always distinguishes in order to unite.

74   Thomas Aquinas, *De ente et essentia,* 5-6.

75   This definition comes in response to the question "What is sexuality?" as given by the Gender Relations Center at the University of Notre Dame, in its 2009 brochure.

76   J. Budziszewski, *The Line through the Heart. Natural Law as Fact, Theory, and Sign of Contradiction* (Wilmington, DE: ISI Books, 2009), 50; and *On the Meaning of Sex* (Wilmington, DE: ISI Books, 2012), 22; emphasis his.

77   Georges Cottier, *Défis éthiques* (Saint-Maurice, Switzerland:

Editions Saint-Augustin, 1996), 25.

78 By marriage, of course, we mean the union of a man and a woman, since only this union is procreative by design. No matter if circumstances sometimes impede the realization of the procreative ordering, such as in the case of hormonal imbalance, advanced age, the infertile phase of the menstrual cycle, etc., the sexual union of man and woman, husband and wife, remains at all points, at the very least symbolically, ordered to procreation. If heterosexual coitus fails to attain the procreative end to which nature orders it, it is merely for circumstantial reasons. This is different in kind from a sexual union, like a homosexual one, that is not by design ordered to procreation, or one that, through contraception, removes the procreative ordering.

79 Aquinas, *Summa Contra Gentiles*, III, 123.

80 John Paul II, *Man and Woman He Created Them: A Theology of the Body*, trans. Michael Waldstein (Boston: Pauline Books, 2006), 184.

81 Russell Hittinger, "Technology and the Demise of Liberalism," in *The First Grace. Rediscovering the Natural Law in a Post-Christian World* (Wilmington, DE: ISI Books, 2003), 256-62. See Wendell Berry, "Feminism, the Body, and the Machine," 190-1.

82 This quote, from the anthropologist Montagu, can be found in Mary Shivanandan, *Crossing the Threshold of Love: A New Vision of Marriage* (The Catholic University of America Press, 1999), p. 178, footnote 5. She cites p. 13 of his book *Sex, Man and Society* (G.P. Putnam's Sons, 1969). One scholar argues, however, that "the liberalization of abortion policy," rather than "pill technology," was what had such a major societal effect on delayed motherhood. I would add that when a woman is pregnant, she is, of course, *already a mother*. See Caitlin Knowles Myers, "The Power of Abortion Policy: Re-examining the effects of young women's access to reproductive control," February 3, 2017, http://community.middlebury. edu/~cmyers/Power_JPE.pdf.

83   As the Jewish philosopher-scientist Leon Kass informs us:
     "For truth to tell, victory over mortality is the unstated but
     implicit goal of modern medical science, indeed of the entire
     modern scientific project, to which mankind was summoned
     almost 400 years ago by Francis Bacon and René Descartes.
     They quite consciously trumpeted the conquest of nature for
     the relief of man's estate, and they founded a science whose
     explicit purpose was to reverse the curse laid on Adam and
     Eve, and especially to restore the tree of life, by means of the
     tree of (scientific) knowledge." https://www.firstthings.com/
     article/2001/05/lchaim-and-its-limits-why-not-immortality.

84   See William J. Bennett, *The Index of Leading Cultural Indicators:
     American Society at the End of the Twentieth Century* (updated and
     expanded). (WaterBrook, 2000).

85   See ibid., *The Broken Hearth: Reversing the Moral Collapse of the
     American Family* (Doubleday, 2001).

86   Cf. *Lumen Gentium*, 10, 36. An excellent discussion of this is
     found in the doctoral dissertation of Rev. Lorenzo Manual
     Albacete Cintron, *Human Dominion Over Creation: A Priestly
     Act According to John Paul II* (Washington, DC: 1983, Pontifical
     University of St. Thomas Aquinas, S.T.D. Dissertation).

87   See William E. May, "John Paul II's Catechesis on the
     Theology of the Body," in William E. May, *Marriage: The Rock
     on Which the Family Is Built*, Second edition (Ignatius Press,
     2009), pp. 109-111.

88   See ibid., "Pope Paul VI: True Prophet," in May, *Marriage*, p. 66.

89   Karol Wojytla, "Subjectivity and the Irreducible," in Wojtyla,
     Person and Community, Selected Essays, trans. Theresa Sandok,
     O.S.M. (Peter Lang, 1993), p. 214. Quoted in Peter Bristow,
     *Christian Ethics and the Human Person: Truth and Relativism in
     Contemporary Moral Theology* (Family Publications/Maryvale
     Institute, 2009), pp. 102-103.

90   Bristow, *Christian Ethics and the Human Person*, p. 103.

91   Ibid., p. 102. See also Wojtyla, "Thomistic Personalism," in
     Wojtyla, *Person and Community*, pp. 165-175. One of the best
     treatments of John Paul II's personalism can be found in Kenneth

Schmitz, *At the Center of the Human Drama: The Philosophical Anthropology of Karol Wojtyla/Pope John Paul II* (Washington, DC: The Catholic University of America Press, 1993).

92 Among many who made this bogus claim, the American Joseph Selling was probably the most prominent. See his "Moral Teaching, Traditional Teaching, and *Humanae Vitae*," *Louvain Studies* 7 (1978): 24-44. My response to Selling can be found in my article, "Is the Teaching of *Humanae Vitae* Physicalist? A Critique of the View of Joseph A. Selling," *Linacre Quarterly: A Journal of the Philosophy and Ethics of Medical Practice*, Vol. 62, No. 4 (November 1995): 39-58.

93 "The Anthropological Vision of *Humanae Vitae*," 1978, http://www.christendom-awake.org/pages/may/anthrop-visionjpII.htm, translated from the original Italian by William E. May.

94 Cf. Pope Pius XI, *Casti Connubii*, nos. 53-59, https://w2.vatican.va/content/pius-xi/en/encyclicals/documents/hf_p-xi_enc_19301231_casti-connubii.html; Pope Pius XII, "Address to Midwives," October 29, 1951, https://www.ewtn.com/library/PAPALDOC/P511029.HTM. "Our Predecessor, Pius XI, of happy memory, in his Encyclical *Casti Connubii*, of December 31, 1930, once again solemnly proclaimed the fundamental law of the conjugal act and conjugal relations: that every attempt of either husband or wife in the performance of the conjugal act or in the development of its natural consequences which aims at depriving it of its inherent force and hinders the procreation of new life is immoral; and that no 'indication' or need can convert an act which is intrinsically immoral into a moral and lawful one. This precept is in full force today, as it was in the past, and so it will be in the future also, and always, because it is not a simple human whim, but the expression of a natural and divine law."

95 Many years ago I was in a Catholic bookstore when I overheard two friends joke about the books on Catholic sexual ethics being obviously quite slim!

96 This most basic principle of moral choice is also quite compatible with the biblical command of Jesus to love God

above all else and our neighbor as one's self. See Matthew
22:35-40 and parallels in Mark and Luke.

97   See Mark S. Latkovic, "Moral Judgment," *New Catholic
Encyclopedia Supplement 2012-2013: Ethics and Philosophy*, Vol. 4,
ed. Robert L. Fastiggi (Detroit: Gale, 2013): 1017-1019.

98   Many are once again challenging the notion that contraception is
an intrinsically evil act. See http://magister.blogautore.espresso.
repubblica.it/2018/01/30/goodbye-humanae-vitae-francis-
liberalizes-the-pill/. See also https://www.catholicnewsagency.
com/news/analysis-questioning-humanae-vitae-the-vatican-
has-already-had-its-say-29199. Although, all is not bad news:
https://www.catholicnewsagency.com/news/denver-archbishop-
spotlights-humanae-vitae-in-new-pastoral-letter-49281/.

99   Cf. William E. May, Rev. Ronald Lawler, O.F.M. Cap.,
& Joseph Boyle, Jr., *Catholic Sexual Ethics: A Summary,
Explanation, & Defense*, 3rd Edition (Our Sunday Visitor Press,
2011), pp. 240-243.

100 Polluting neither our oceans with waste hormones nor our
landfills with mounds of latex, NFP is truly "green" family
planning. One would think that the secular mind, with its
concern for the environment, would welcome such a natural
and highly reliable means of "birth control." But the world is
not logical or consistent.

101 Pope John Paul II's encyclical on the Gospel of Life, *Evangelium
Vitae*, provides a marvelous overview of the high value that
both the Old and New Testament place on children, including
the child in the womb. My former student, Laura A. Cristiano
has found a fascinating *biblical* reference to the connection
between the "unitive" and "procreative" goods of sexuality
that is worth noting. This connection, she notes, is "alluded
to by the biblical author of Wisdom, who describes how he
came into being, 'In the womb of a mother I was molded into
flesh . . . from *the seed of a man and the pleasure of marriage*' (Wis.
7:1b, 2b, emphasis added)." She argues that "'The seed of a
man' refers to the procreative meaning of the conjugal act, and
'the pleasure of marriage' refers to the unitive meaning of the

conjugal act." (M.A. Thesis, Sacred Heart Major Seminary, 2010, published as "Abraham, Sarah, and Surrogacy: A Scriptural Insight into Church Teaching," *The National Catholic Bioethics Quarterly*, Vol. 11, No. 3/Autumn 2011: 443-452).

102 I take this holistic anthropology of HV to be one that counters the dualistic anthropology that characterizes our secular culture's view of the human person. In separating the body from the mind (or soul), it sees man's body as merely subpersonal material over which his mind, as the only truly personal reality, must assert itself. Some moral theologians, for example, Eberhard Schockenhoff, *Natural Law & Human Dignity: Universal Ethics in an Historical World* (The Catholic University of America Press, 2003), pp. 202-210 have tried to respond to those who criticize dualism by arguing that "the personal self-experience of the human being also includes the capacity to take up a distance vis-à-vis his own body; in German, one can make this distinction by saying that the *Leib* which we *are* is not identical with the *Körper* which we *have*. This means that the reference to the unity of the person as body and soul does not disqualify every intervention in bodily life as ethically impermissible. Where this unity is proposed in a way that systematically obscures the freedom which the person enjoys vis-à-vis his own body, there are very good reasons for objecting to it." (p. 209). Although Schockenhoff does not in any way deny the importance of our bodily existence, he wants to avoid "dissolving the person's relationship to his own self in his bodily existence into an immediate identity" (p. 209), and thus ultimately leave "wiggle room" for justifying acts such as contraception. He also thinks that traditionalist defenders of magisterial teaching do not allow for artificial or technological interventions on the human person (see p. 208, footnote 130). But this is false. They actually do allow it in principle, but it all depends on what *kind* of intervention, regardless of its "artificiality." Is it a pacemaker or the Pill? The latter is immoral, the former is not.

103 See especially the work of Thomas W. Hilgers, M.D. and the

Pope Paul VI Institute for the Study of Human Reproduction
in Omaha, NE (https://www.popepaulvi.com/). They have
developed the Creighton Model Fertility Care System and
NaPro Technology.

104 Pope John Paul II will also speak of the body as a "sign" or
"sacrament" of the person. The "*language of the body*" argument,
developed especially by John Paul II in his "Theology
of the Body" audiences, is strong: contraceptive sex and
noncontraceptive sex, or sex open to babies, "say" or "express"
two very different things. The sexual act is an *expressive* act;
by its very nature it expresses a willingness to be a parent with
another. Contraceptors *falsify* that "speech," telling "lies" with
their bodies. That is, their bodies do not speak the *truth* of
human sexuality: they are not saying with their bodies that they
are willing to be parents with each other; they are saying only
that they want to experience a great pleasure or intimacy with
each other (see Pope John Paul II, *Familiaris Consortio*, no. 32).
Even if they subjectively intend to say more, their contraceptive
acts *cannot* say more; they can speak only the desire to have
a momentary physical union with another (although, with
contraception, even that physical union is not total or complete).
On the other hand, noncontraceptors are saying with their
sexual acts: "I am willing to procreate with you; to help create
another 'you' (and 'me'). I want to have an unlimited future
and an irrevocable bond with you. I want to be an irreplaceable,
non-substitutable, and non-disposable person in your life."
This is a powerful personalist argument that I believe can
"speak" to today's young couples. I will say more about John
Paul II's Theology of the Body, especially its argument against
contraception and support for HV, in Part IX.

105 Alain Mattheeuws, *Les "dons" du mariage: Recherche de théologie
morale et sacramentelle*, p. 12, quoted in Angelo Cardinal Scola,
The Nuptial Mystery (Wm. B. Eerdmans Pub., 2005), p. 203,
footnote 60.

106 John Finnis, "Personal Integrity, Sexual Morality and
Responsible Parenthood," *Anthropos* 1 (1985): 43-55; reprinted

in Janet E. Smith (ed.), *Why Humane Vitae Was Right: A Reader* (Ignatius Press, 1993), pp. 173-192, at p. 185. Finnis speaks of the "conjugal good" as a "complex good" that is a "friendship" and "procreative." (pp. 184-185). In this article, Finnis develops a fascinating argument against contraception: it "settles for the appearance rather than the reality (at the expense of the more arduously attainable reality)," i.e., it is "a simulation of *conjugal* intercourse . . ." (p. 188).

107 John Kippley, in his *Sex and the Marriage Covenant: A Basis for Morality* (Couple to Couple League, 1991) develops an argument against contraception based on its incompatibility with the marriage covenant.

108 As the secular state began to assert its power over marriage against the Church, the popes of the past few centuries have been tireless in reminding us that "God is the author of marriage."

109 This obviously could be the subject of another article. A sound treatment of conscience—its meaning, formation, and relationship to Church authority—can be found in May, Lawler, and Boyle, *Catholic Sexual Ethics*, Ch. Five. See also my "The Primacy of Conscience, the Synod and the Catholic Faith," October 20, 2015, http://www.ncregister.com/daily-news/propagating-the-primacy-of-conscience-error.

110 George Weigel, "*Humanae Vitae* at Forty," https://eppc.org/publications/humanae-vitae-at-forty/.

111 Note these words of *Gaudium et Spes*, no. 51: "All should be persuaded that human life and the task of transmitting it are not realities bound up with this world alone. Hence they cannot be measured or perceived only in terms of it, but always have a bearing on the eternal destiny of men."

112 See also the fascinating article by John Haas, president of the National Catholic Bioethics Center and a former Protestant: https://www.crisismagazine.com/1989/straight-talk-about-contraception-the-churchs-yes-to-the-gift-of-life.

113 "If I Were Pope . . . ," *National Review,* June 9, 1978, p. 706.

114 "Message of His Holiness Benedict XVI on the Occasion of the Fortieth Anniversary of Paul VI's Encyclical *Humanae Vitae*,"

https://w2.vatican.va/content/benedict-xvi/en/messages/pont-messages/2008/documents/hf_ben-xvi_mes_20081002_isi.html.

115 Cf. *Evangelium Vitae* 13.

116 William E. May shows, against Fr. Curran, just in fact how personalistic *Humanae Vitae* really is, in his "The Moral Methodology of Vatican Council II and the Teaching of *Humanae Vitae* and *Persona Humana*," *Anthropotes: Rivista di Studi sulla Persona e la Famiglia* 5.1 (1989): 29-46.

117 See VS, Ch. 2, Part I, "Freedom and Law," nos. 35-53, especially 46-50 that deals with the physicalism charge and the place of the human body in morality.

118 In footnote 86, the pope cites "Cf. Ecumenical Council of Vienne, Constitution *Fidei Catholicae*: DS, 902; Fifth Lateran Ecumenical Council, Bull *Apostolici Regiminis*: DS, 1440." In footnote 87, he cites the "Second Vatican Ecumenical Council, Pastoral Constitution on the Church in the Modern World *Gaudium et Spes*, 14." I would note here that many of the theologians that fall prey to relativism highlight the importance of the "historicity" of human existence as part of their "historically minded" worldview (as opposed to a "classicist" worldview, which they reject). Of course, we are historical beings who live only in history. But unfortunately, these theologians go from historicity to *historicism*. And the latter view is simply relativistic.

119 See also VS, no. 13 for evidence of John Paul II's personalistic understanding of the natural law: "The commandments of which Jesus reminds the young man are meant to safeguard *the good* of the person, the image of God, by protecting his *goods*. 'You shall not murder; You shall not commit adultery; You shall not steal; You shall not bear false witness' are moral rules formulated in terms of prohibitions. These negative precepts express with particular force the ever urgent need to protect human life, the communion of persons in marriage, private property, truthfulness and people's good name." One should also cite here Karol Wojtyla/Pope John Paul II's "personalistic norm": "This norm, in its negative

aspect, states that the person is the kind of good which does not admit of use and cannot be treated as an object of use and as such the means to an end. In its positive form the personalistic norm confirms this: the person is a good toward which the only proper and adequate attitude is love." *Love and Responsibility* (Ignatius Press, 1993; originally published in 1960), p. 41. As I noted in Part II, not all versions of personalism are sound. Some are revisionist and thus support positions at odds with magisterial teaching. See, for example, Jan Jans, "Personalism: The Foundations of an Ethics of Responsibility," *Ethical Perspectives* 3 (1996): 148-156, which relies on the thought of the proportionalist Belgian priest-moral theologian, Louis Janssens (1908-2001), http://www.ethical-perspectives.be/viewpic.php?TABLE=EP&ID=852.

120 On the issue of contraception, GS, no. 51 is an important text: "To these problems [of married life] there are those who presume to offer dishonorable solutions indeed; they do not recoil even from the taking of life. But the Church issues the reminder that a true contradiction cannot exist between the divine laws pertaining to the transmission of life and those pertaining to authentic conjugal love . . . Hence *when there is question of harmonizing conjugal love with the responsible transmission of life, the moral aspects of any procedure does not depend solely on sincere intentions or on an evaluation of motives, but must be determined by objective standards. These, based on the nature of the human person and his acts, preserve the full sense of mutual self-giving and human procreation in the context of true love.* Such a goal cannot be achieved unless the virtue of conjugal chastity is sincerely practiced. Relying on these principles, sons of the Church may not undertake methods of birth control which are found blameworthy by the teaching authority of the Church in its unfolding of the divine law." Emphasis added.

121 In endnote 90, the pope cites the "Congregation for the Doctrine of the Faith, Instruction on Respect for Human Life in its Origin and on the Dignity of Procreation *Donum Vitae* (February 22, 1987), Introduction, 3: *AAS* 80 (1988), 74;

cf. Paul VI, Encyclical Letter *Humanae Vitae* (July 25, 1968),
10: *AAS* 60 (1968), pp. 487-488."

122 John Paul II, *Man and Woman He Created Them,* trans. Michael
Waldstein, p. 619, cited in May, *Marriage*, p. 133.

123 Ibid., p. 631, cited in May, *Marriage*, p. 133.

124 May, *Marriage*, p. 133. May cites p. 632 of Waldstein's
translation, *Man and Woman He Created Them.*

125 John Paul II, *Man and Woman He Created Them*, p. 632, cited in
May, *Marriage*, p. 133. Emphasis added.

126 Ibid., p. 633, cited in May, *Marriage*, pp. 133-134. For another
defense of HV along personalist grounds, see Dietrich
Von Hildebrand, *The Encyclical Humanae Vitae: A Sign of
Contradiction* (Franciscan Press, 1969).

127 See http://www.janetesmith.com/.

128 See http://epublications.marquette.edu/cgi/viewcontent.cgi?art
icle=1008&context=nursing_fac.

129 I am aware of the many writings today by Catholics who are
critical of aspects of NFP, although they are trying to abide
by the Church's teaching. They try to "de-romanticize" what
they see as an overly "rosy" picture of NFP on the part of some
Catholics. Or some will even imply that using NFP makes
one less than a "hard-core Catholic"—a sort of "Catholic
lightweight" in their eyes.

130 Cardinal Joseph Ratzinger, *Homily: Pro Eligendo Romano
Pontifice*, April 18, 2005.

131 Paul VI, *Humane Vitae*, Section 21.

132 Robin Lane Fox, *Pagans and Christians* (New York: Alfred A.
Knopf, 1987), 341.

133 Ibid., 342.

134 The poet Horace argued that "young men should drop in
there, rather than grind some husband's private mill."

135 Rodney Stark, *The Rise of Christianity: A Sociologist Reconsiders
History* (Princeton, NJ: Princeton University Press, 1996), 97.

136 On the Romans, see: Robin Fox Lane, *Pagans and Christians*
(New York: Alfred A. Knopf, 1987), 340-64; Tim G. Parkin,
Demography and Roman Society (Baltimore, MO: The Johns

Hopkins University Press, 1992), 110-33; A.T. Sandison, "Sexual Behavior in Ancient Societies," in Don Brothwell and A.T. Sandison, eds., Diseases in Antiquity (Springfield, IL: Charles C. Thomas, 1967), 734-43: and Arthur E.R. Boak, Manpower Shortage and the Fall of the Roman Empire in the West (Ann Arbor: University of Michigan Press, 1955), 49-54, 109-29.

137 Ibid., 107.

138 On the sexual ethic of the early Christians, see: Robert L. Wilken, The Christians as the Romans Saw Them (New Haven, CT: Yale University Press, 1984), 31-47; Rodney Stark, The Rise of Christianity: A Sociologist Reconsiders History (Princeton, NJ: Princeton University Press, 1996), 95-128; Rodney Stark, Cities of God: The Real Story of How Christianity Became An Urban Movement and Conquered Rome (New York: Harper Collins, 2006), 64-70: and Michael J. Gorman, Abortion and the Early Church: Christian, Jewish & Pagan Attitudes in the Greco-Roman World (Downers Grove, IL: Intervarsity Press, 1982), 48-62.

139 Giovanni Filorama, *A History of Gnosticism* (Oxford: Basil Blackwell, 1990), 183-84.

140 John T. Noonan, Jr., *Contraception: A History of Its Treatment by the Catholic Theologians and Canonists* (Cambridge, MA: The Belknap Press of Harvard University Press, 1986), 60-61.

141 Robert M. Grant, *Gnosticism: A Source Book of Heretical Writings from the Early Christian Period* (New York: Harper and Brothers, 1959), 47-48.

142 Ibid, 179-199.

143 Luther's Works, Vol. 5, 117-18, 133; Vol. 45, 18, 21, 41.

144 John Calvin, Commentary on Genesis, Vol. 2, part 16, 8-9.

145 Fox, *Pagans and Christians*, 341.

146 The full story is found in: Allan Carlson, *Godly Seed: American Evangelicals Confront Birth Control, 1873-1973* (New Brunswick, NJ: Transaction, 2012), 79-108.

147 John A. Ryan, "Family Limitation," *The Ecclesiastical Review* 4 (June 1916), 684-96.

148 From: Kathleen A. Tobin, *The American Religious Debate*

over Birth Control, 1907-1937 (Jefferson, NC and London: McFarland, 2001), 77-83.

149 Post-millennialism is the eschatological view that human actions and social reforms done now can help inaugurate the millennium, a blessed time that will establish the kingdom of God on earth and culminate in Christ's second coming.

150 Kenneth C. MacArthur, "Eugenics and the Church;" *Eugenics* 1 (December 1928), 6-9.

151 From: Richard M. Fagley, *The Population Explosion and Christian Responsibility* (New York: Oxford University, 1960), 203.

152 Ibid., 233.

153 "Responsible Parenthood and the Population Problem," appendix to Fagley, *Population Explosion and Christian Responsibility,* 226-29.

154 George Dugan, "Graham Sees Hope in Birth Control," *The New York Times*, December 13, 1959.

155 "A Protestant Affirmation on the Control of Human Reproduction," *Christianity Today* 13 (November 8, 1968), 18-19.

156 John Warwick Montgomery, "How to Decide the Birth Control Question," *Christianity Today* 10 (March 10, 1966), 10.

157 John Warwick Montgomery, "The Christian View of The Fetus," in *Birth Control and the Christians*, eds. Walter O. Spitzer and Carlyle L. Saylor (Wheaton, IL: Tyndale House, 1969), 176-87.

158 Allan Sherman, *The Rape of the A★P★E★: The Official History of the Sex Revolution* (Chicago: Playboy Press, 1973), 7, 73-75, 389.

159 *Casti Connubii*: Encyclical Letter of Pope Pius XI on Christian Marriage.

160 Alberts Cavallari, *The Changing Vatican* (New York: Doubleday 1967), 186-87.

161 Robert McClory, *Turning Point: The Inside Story of the Papal Birth Control Commission* (New York: Crossroad, 1995), 78.

162 Appendix I: "Responsible Parenthood: Majority Report of the Birth Control Commission; in McClory, Turning Point, 171-87. Emphasis added.

163 Sex in Marriage, 1, 37.

164 "The Church and Contraception," 11.

165 "Example," 2.

166 Ibid., 4, 7.

167 Ibid., 2-3.

168 Richard J. Fehring, "The Influence of Contraception, Abortion, and Natural Family Planning on Divorce Rates as Found in the 2006-2010 National Survey of Family Growth," Linacre Quarterly 82.3 (2015), 273-82.

169 Lionel Tiger, *The Decline of Males. The First Look at an Unexpected New World for Men and Women* (New York: St. Martin's Griffin, 1999), 29-60.

170 George A. Akerlof, Janet L. Yellen, and Michael L. Katz, "An Analysis of Out-of-Wedlock Child Bearing in the United States, *The Quarterly Journal of Economics* 111, No. 2 (May 1996), 277-317. Emphasis added.

171 Alexandra Alvergne and Virpi Lummaa, "Does the Contraceptive Pill Alter Mate Choice in Humans," Trends in Ecology and Evolution 25, No. 3 (2009), 171-79. Emphasis added.

172 Claudia Goldin and Lawrence F. Katz, "The Power of the Pill: Oral Contraceptives and Women's Career and Marriage Decisions." Working Paper 7527 (Cambridge, MA: National Bureau of Economic Research, 2000), 29-30.

173 Hanna Klaus and Manuel E. Cortes, "Psychological, Social, and Spiritual Effects of Contraceptive Steroid Hormones," *The Linacre Quarterly* 82 (August 2015), 283-300.

174 Matthew Connelly, *Fatal Misconception: The Struggle to Control World Population* (Cambridge, MA: The Belknap Press of Harvard University, 2008), 14, 296.

175 *National Catholic Reporter*, August 7, 1968.